BUSINESS MODELS IN EUROPEAN BANKING

A PRE-AND POST-CRISIS SCREENING

RYM AYADI
EMRAH ARBAK
WILLEM PIETER DE GROEN

WITH A CONTRIBUTION FROM
DAVID T. LLEWELLYN

CENTRE FOR EUROPEAN POLICY STUDIES
BRUSSELS

The Centre for European Policy Studies (CEPS) is an independent policy research institute based in Brussels. Its mission is to produce sound analytical research leading to constructive solutions to the challenges facing Europe today. CEPS Paperbacks present analysis and views by leading experts on important questions in the arena of European public policy, written in a style geared to an informed but generalist readership.

This study was commissioned by the Greens-European Free Alliance Political Group in the European Parliament and directed by Dr. Rym Ayadi, Senior Research Fellow and Head of the Financial Institutions and Prudential Policy research unit at CEPS. The research team included Emrah Arbak, Researcher and Willem Pieter de Groen, Research Assistant in the same unit at CEPS. An overall review and written contributions, including the Foreword, from David T. Llewellyn of Loughborough University, the Cass Business School in London and the Vienna University of Economics and Business Administration, are gratefully acknowledged. The authors also acknowledge useful comments and suggestions by Rudi Vander Vennet, Professor of Financial Economics at the University of Ghent.

The aim of the study is to examine the key business models adopted by the most prominent EU banks in the period leading up to, during and immediately following the financial crisis, with a view to identifying key weaknesses inherent in these models in light of upcoming regulatory changes.

The views expressed in this report are those of the authors writing in a personal capacity and do not necessarily reflect those of CEPS or any other institution with which they are associated.

Centre for European Policy Studies
Place du Congrès 1, B-1000 Brussels
Tel: 32 (0) 2 229.39.11 Fax: 32 (0) 2 219.41.51
e-mail: info@ceps.eu
internet: http://www.ceps.eu

CONTENTS

FOREWORD

Two important and related perspectives are offered at the outset of this review of an important new study by the Centre for European Policy Studies. First, the performance and efficiency of the banking sector has a major impact on a country's overall efficiency and economic performance, and second, for several European banks, business models changed markedly in the years running up to the banking crisis and are currently in a state of flux. Business models will continue to evolve in the post-crisis scenario. In this context, CEPS' report on contrasting business models of banks and an assessment of their implications could not be more timely. The report offers a unique and comprehensive empirical study of different bank business models and their implications for risk characteristics, systemic stability, bank performance, efficiency and governance issues.

The report gives the results of the first screening exercise of the business models of 26 major European banks before and after the crisis. On the basis of state-of-the-art methodology and detailed statistical analysis, the authors find that three major alternative business models can be identified:

- *Retail banks:* those using customer deposits as the primary source of funding and providing predominantly customer loans (this group kept fairly close to the traditional banking model);
- *Investment banks:* those with substantial trading and derivatives activity; and
- *Wholesale banks:* those institutions that are active in wholesale and interbank markets with a focus on domestic business.

The 26 large banks and banking groups in the sample accounted for 55% of total EU banking assets. The period covered was 2006-09, giving 108 bank-year observations. A wide range of performance and other indicators was used related to structure, ownership, financial activity, financial performance, risk, impact of the crisis and governance issues.

The study was carried out in four stages. Firstly, the sample of banks was selected, based largely on the availability of data for large banks. The second stage involved the creation of a large database in order to construct a picture of business models, profitability, asset and liability structure, earnings performance, stability and governance aspects for each of the banks in the sample. This created over 200 variables for each bank/year observation. The third stage involved identifying different business models, using cluster analysis methodology. The business models are distinguished largely in terms of the banks' scope of activities and funding strategies. In the fourth stage, the three identified business models were evaluated and compared for relative performance, riskiness, governance and other relevant dimensions.

On the basis of a new and comprehensive data set, the report identifies a credible and extremely useful categorisation of alternative business models, based on a sound methodology, namely:

- There is a unique and systematic analysis of the implications of alternative business models in five main dimensions: risk characteristics, systemic stability, bank performance, efficiency and corporate governance. The report provides an excellent survey of the positive and negative aspects of different business models.

- Advances are made in methodology and statistical testing, which add to our understanding of bank performance and behaviour.

- The analysis in the report highlights some important regulatory implications of different bank business models.

- The study offers valuable insights into how the crisis differentially impacted on banks with different business models, with retail banks being affected less than the other two models, especially in comparison with the wholesale bank model. The results of the analysis provide some rationale for the recent popularisation of the retail banking model, and may also suggest some regulatory implications for the future.

Overall, the results show that the performance of retail banks has in general been superior to the other two models. They were also less prone to the need for state support during the crisis. In terms of one of the two perspectives outlined at the beginning of this review, the report finds that retail banks continued to support the economy by continuing to extend loans to customers.

This pioneering study contains the results of the first screening of European banks' business models over the period 2006-09. In the process, the research has developed a powerful methodology for analysing bank business models and bank performance and risk on a continuing basis. Several advantages would emerge from future research that would be of value to banks, regulators and analysts:

- The coverage of banks could be usefully extended, and the methodology could be further refined.

- The analysis in the report also highlights important areas where more disclosure is needed, especially with regard to banks' risk exposures.

- The report correctly identifies that the post-crisis scenario will witness transformational changes in bank business models and in the conduct of regulation and supervision, the implications of which will affect not only banks and the banking sector, but also the wider economy.

In a period of profound change, which the post-crisis scenario is likely to be, it is important to have a clear, comprehensive and consistent methodology for monitoring what banks do and how their business models change over time.

David T. Llewellyn
Professor of Money and Banking
Loughborough University

1. INTRODUCTION

O ver the next few years, Europe's financial regulatory framework is likely to experience one of the biggest changes it has ever faced, which will undoubtedly have a major impact on many aspects of banking and banking models in the EU. In the aftermath of the 2007-09 financial crisis, the coming years promise to be crucial, with the adoption of a number of financial sector reforms within the European Union. Among the packages currently on the table, a substantial piece of legislation is the amended Capital Requirements Directive, or the so-called 'CRD IV'. The revisions will complement the recent changes that aimed to strengthen the capital and disclosure requirements for the trading book and re-securitisation instruments as well as restrictions to ensure that remuneration policies do not lead to excessive risk-taking. More specifically, the new amendments will translate the Basel III revisions that were adopted in September 2010 by the Basel Committee on Banking Supervision (BCBS) into European law, tightening the existing capital requirements; introduce new rules on liquidity, leverage ratios, counter-cyclical measures and systemically important financial institutions; and amend the definition of capital, counterparty credit risk and rules for banking book. Most of these changes will be phased-in gradually between now and 2019. Banks will have to respond by adapting their business models to the new regulatory environment.

This report provides the results of a first screening exercise of the business models, performance, risk and governance of 26 major European banks before and after the crisis. One of our main findings is that the banks sampled appear to follow one of three distinct business models. The banks identified as 'retail banks' have remained close to their original traditional banking model, using customer deposits as their primary source of funding and providing predominantly customer loans, with limited trading exposures. Banks in the second distinct category, the so-called 'investment banks', are more engaged in trading activities, especially in derivatives transactions. Due to the inherent volatility of these securities, these banks are more likely to actively manage their balance sheets to mop up any excess capacity, relying on short-term funding sources. The third category consists of what can be loosely called 'wholesale banks'. In comparison with their peers, these banks are more active in the interbank markets and remain mostly domestic.

The results show that the performance of retail banks has been in general better than all other banks. Despite their relative size, these traditional banks exhibit commendable stability and have been less likely to receive state support. Moreover, the retail banks in our sample have continued to support the economy by extending their customer loans, despite the crisis. In turn, the wholesale banks are performing possibly the worst, and hence are the most likely to receive state support. Investment banks remain in between these two extremes, although their performance is likely to be comparable to or possibly better than that of retail banks in the pre-crisis years.

This report does not intend to serve as an exhaustive impact assessment, but it nevertheless aims to anticipate and offer insights into the likely results of the forthcoming regulatory changes. The material is organised into seven chapters and as many annexes. Following this introduction, Chapter 2 delves into the reasons why banks' business models evolved as they did in the aftermath of the financial crisis. Chapter 3 provides a comprehensive review of the literature about business models and risk-taking. Chapter 4 outlines the sample of banks studied and the methodology employed. Chapters 5 and 6 present the results and conclusions and finally a concluding chapter looks at changing business models of banks in the post-crisis period and speculates on the potential regulatory implications. Most of the appendices provide supporting technical information about the banks surveyed and our methodology. Appendix III contains a brief profile of each of the 26 banks surveyed, containing a description of their activities, a listing of any state aid received and the ensuing restructuring/expansion.

2. CHANGING BUSINESS MODELS OF EUROPEAN BANKS

Over the past few decades, prior to the onset of the banking crisis, several structural features of the global banking environment changed, producing major changes in bank business models across Europe and also worldwide. Finance in general, and banking in particular, as an industry expanded substantially and unsustainably ('excessive financialisation'). The role of banks in the financial system increased, banks and financial markets became more closely linked and integrated and business models changed in several important ways. It is likely, however, that many of these changes will now be reversed in the post-crisis scenario.

Traditionally, banks have performed fundamental economic roles, mainly as liquidity providers, maturity transformers, risk managers and financial innovators. Depending on how properly they perform these roles during the macroeconomic cycle, they either become shock absorbers or on the contrary shock originators – as was the case during the financial crisis.

Over the last decades, signs of 'excessive financialisation' were manifested in numerous dimensions: the increasing role of banks in the financial intermediation process, a sharp rise in the assets of the banking system relative to GDP, the rapid growth and overall size of the financial system in the economy, the burgeoning leverage of banks and the overall debt-to-GDP levels in the economy, the degree of intra-sector leverage (the extent to which leverage increased within the financial sector as financial institutions became increasingly exposed to each other), the frenetic pace of financial innovation, the sharp rise in trading volumes of banks, the market capitalisation of banks relative to overall market capitalisation of stock market companies and the share of total profits in the economy accounted for by banks.

Several factors lay behind the financialisation process in the years leading up to the crisis:

- Excess leverage and an under-capitalisation meant that banks could expand at a faster rate and to a higher level than would have been possible had they maintained a level of capital commensurate with their risks. Overall, banks became highly leveraged with a rise in assets on the balance sheet relative to total capital (Alessandri & Haldane, 2009; Wehinger, 2008).

- The systematic under-estimation and under-pricing of risks due to the macroeconomic environment and the collective euphoria of the pre-crisis years increased both the demand for loans and the willingness of banks to meet that demand to maintain an upward cycle.

- The collective euphoria and the high profitability of banks at the time meant that the cost of capital was artificially low because it did not reflect the true risks that banks were incurring. This amounted to an effective subsidy. A perceived safety-net for banks also had the effect of lowering banks' cost of funding.

- For various reasons, including the nature of the competitive environment at the time, banks adopted more short-term strategies to maximise the rate of return on equity. In truth, profitability was enhanced not by superior banking performance, but by banks raising their risk threshold and moving up the risk ladder. Internal reward and bonus structures created a bias towards short-termism and also towards excess risk-taking (Llewellyn, 2010).

Each of these factors, both individually but especially in combination, created sufficient conditions for an over-expansion of banking activity and an artificially enhanced role of banks and other non-regulated financial institutions in the intermediation process.

Several structural changes in the global financial system set the background to the financial crisis and brought about the emergence of new business models in banking.

A defining feature of financial history since the early 1990s was the sharp rise in the pace of financial innovation, and especially in the use of credit derivatives designed to shift credit risk away from loan originators. A major feature of the pre-crisis period was a massive rise in the volume of trading in complex, and sometimes opaque, derivatives contracts. The Bank for International Settlements (BIS) has estimated that the notional amounts outstanding of over-the-counter (OTC) credit default swap (CDS) contracts rose to around $60 trillion by December 2007. One of the factors precipitating the crisis was the exposure of banks to large holdings of securities that were hard to value given the absence of liquid markets. In fact, many credit derivatives were hardly ever traded on any significant scale. Banks became exposed to capital markets and securities trading risks that they did not themselves manage or sometimes truly understand. In addition, over time, banks' holdings of liquid assets fell and their reliance on wholesale markets for liquidity and funding requirements increased.

Another feature is the more market-centric structure of financial systems, which implied a rise in the role of financial markets relative to institutions in the financial intermediation process. Furthermore, banks and markets became increasingly integrated (Boot & Thakor, 2009). One of the many implications of this trend was that losses incurred in markets were at times translated into funding problems for banks. Furthermore, financial systems became more susceptible to market shocks, particularly in a continuous increase in interconnectedness and network externalities.[1]

---

[1] Haldane (2009) defines the network as being both *complex* and *adaptive*: complex by virtue of the many interconnections within the network, and adaptive in that behaviour is driven by the interactions between optimising agents. He describes trends in the network as increased connectivity, there being a small number of hubs with multiple spokes, and the average path length within the network became shorter over time, leading to a small number of degrees of separation between countries and institutions. As a result, comparatively small shocks can have large systemic implications. Several factors contributed to the rise in network externalities, including the enhanced trading in derivatives (and credit derivatives in particular), the growing links between instruments and institutions, the increased globalisation of finance, the trend towards de-regulation, banks diversifying into a wider range of business lines and into securities trading in particular, the growing homogeneity of banks in their business models, and the greater use by banks of wholesale market funding. Each of these trends had the effect of increasing the degree of connectedness between institutions and, as a result, the potential power of network externalities. Increased connectivity also complicated the monitoring of indirect counterparty risks. While bank A may be able to monitor its individual exposure to bank B, it becomes increasingly complex when bank B has a multitude of exposures within the network via derivatives and contingent liabilities, as this gives rise to indirect counterparty risks originating elsewhere in the network.

Network externalities and the increasing connectedness of financial institutions with each other and with markets increased sharply in the years prior to the crisis. In the process, banks became exposed to capital market risks that they did not themselves manage or, in some cases, even understand. This increased connectedness meant that the number of banks that became potentially 'systemically significantly' increased. The increased connectedness arose through many channels, including, inter alia increased exposures in the inter-bank market, banks buying credit risk-shifting instruments and other derivatives issued by other banks, all banks trading in the same instruments and the reduced systemic diversity as banks adopted similar business models.

To complete the picture, largely unregulated 'shadow banks', such as hedge funds and structured investment vehicles (SIVs) emerged as major new players in the financial intermediation process (Tett, 2008) with all the risks and new sources of instabilities they bring.

The nature of bank risks also changed. Securitisation and other credit derivatives were designed specifically to shift credit risk and, for some years, they did just that. However, they also changed the nature of risk and, in particular, transformed credit risk into liquidity risk (buyers of the securities issued to purchase securitised assets from banks being unable to trade them), then into a funding risk (the securitising banks being unable to either sell assets at other than fire-sale prices or roll-over maturing debt), and ultimately into a solvency risk. The latter arose because banks were unable to sell assets in order to continue funding their securitisation programmes.

A defining structural change was the combination of increased diversification and reduced diversity. In many ways, financial firms became less differentiated in that they followed a common policy of diversification, applied new business models, used similar risk analysis models and developed rates of return on equity strategies more forcefully.

As a consequence, banks developed new business models and moved away from their traditional model of 'originate-to-hold', whereby banks issue loans and hold the risk in their books. The emergence of new business models focused largely, though not entirely, on new credit risk-shifting instruments. Several trends in bank business models emerged in the years leading up to the crisis:

- Banks increasingly diversified into more lines of business activity, some of which had previously been prohibited by regulation.

- Securitisation of loans became a central business strategy for many banks.

- Investment and trading activity increased sharply, and the proportion of traded assets in the total balance sheet rose substantially in many cases.

- Banks reduced their holdings of liquid assets as they developed greater access to wholesale funding markets.

- The extent of maturity transformation also increased sharply as greater use was made of short-maturity money market funding sources.

- An increased dependency developed on wholesale and money market funding.

- A powerful trend emerged towards using credit derivatives as a means of shifting credit risk (a notion was called into question during the crisis).

It is instructive to begin with a stylised review of the traditional model of the banking firm (see Llewellyn, 1999, for a fuller discussion). Banks traditionally have information, risk analysis and monitoring advantages, which enable them to solve asymmetric information problems and hence mitigate *adverse selection* and *moral hazard*. Banks accept deposits and utilise their comparative advantages to transform deposits into loans. In this model, the bank accepts the credit (default) risk, holds the asset on its own balance sheet, monitors its borrowing customers and holds appropriate levels of capital to cover unexpected risk. It also effectively 'insures' its loans internally through the risk premia incorporated into the rate of interest on loans. In this process, the bank offers an integrated service in that it performs all the core functions in the financial intermediation process.

Furthermore, in this traditional model, the bank is not able to shift credit risk to other agents because of its asymmetric information advantages: a potential buyer or insurer of a loan from a bank might judge that, because of the bank's information advantage, there is an *adverse selection* and *moral hazard* problem in that the bank might select low-quality loans to pass on and, if it knew that it could pass on risk, it might be less careful in assessing the risk of new loans and would conduct less-intensive monitoring of borrowers after loans have been made. For the same reason, the traditional view of the bank is that it is unable to externally insure its credit risks and instead applies a risk (insurance) premium on loans and holds capital as an internal insurance fund. The reason for this outcome is that, given the uncertainties outlined above, an external insurer would reflect this uncertainty in the insurance premium charged to the bank. In this traditional view of the bank, therefore, credit risk cannot be shifted or insured, there is no liquidity in bank loans and banks are locked into their loan portfolios.

However, many aspects of this traditional model came to be questioned. In the securitisation model, the process of securitisation (including via collateralised debt obligations or CDOs) means that the bank is able to sell loans (which the traditional model denies) and hence the bank does not hold the loan asset on its own balance sheet and does not absorb the credit risk. Hence it does not need to hold capital against the credit risk. However, this depends precisely upon how the securitisation is conducted and especially whether the SPV (special purpose vehicle) is truly bankruptcy-remote from the bank and vice versa.

The CDS model is similar to the securitisation model except that, while the credit risk is passed to the protection seller, the asset remains on the balance sheet of the originating bank. In this model there is explicit external insurance of bank loans.

These business alterations to the traditional model of the banking firm meant that banks were no longer required to perform all the functions in the bank intermediation process. Furthermore, banks were also able to outsource some of their other activities such as loan administration, credit assessment through credit-scoring models of other banks, etc. This further challenged the traditional view of the integrated bank. Banking was no longer a totally integrated process whereby a bank conducts all the functions in the loan process. Credit risk transfer facilities and instruments changed the relationship between borrowers and lenders and created different incentive structures than had been present in the traditional model of the banking firm. As a result, banks stopped behaving in the traditional way as market-makers in credit risk and, in effect, came to act as brokers in credit risk between ultimate borrowers and those who either purchased asset-backed securities or who offered CDS insurance. Therefore, the balance sheets of banks no longer provide the real picture of banks' activities as the off-balance sheet became ever more important.

3. THE LITERATURE ON BUSINESS MODELS OF BANKS

Economic literature provides several reasons why banks may choose to diversify their business models instead of specialising in a narrow range of activities. This is seen, for instance, in the *bancassurance* model, which became common in many European countries. First, by providing a service, banks gain valuable information on their clients that might provide advantages in the provision of other services (Sharpe, 1990; Diamond, 1991; Rajan, 1992). Second, by engaging in a wide range of activities, banks may also reduce their risks through diversification and economies of scope (Diamond, 1984). Lastly, as regulatory reforms diminish competitive inequalities, banks with different models compete with one another, providing incentives to offer a broader range of products to their customers. Many banks have also adjusted their business profiles to reflect changes in the demographic structure of their retail client base.

Although diversification may prove beneficial to the bank, it may also endanger social welfare. A typical bank-client relationship can harbour a variety of conflicts of interests, providing informational advantages to banks vis-à-vis the market. For example, first-hand information on borrowers may enable a bank to extract monopolistic rents to 'lock-in' the customer to its services in the future (Sharpe, 1990; Rajan, 1992). These incumbent advantages may hinder competition in the market by acting as barriers to entry (Dell'Ariccia et al., 1999; Marquez, 2002). Alternatively, confronted with exclusive information about the financial health of their clients, banks may underwrite a troubled firm's securities despite known risks, in an attempt to secure the repayment of earlier loans (Kanatas & Qi, 1998).

The potential for conflicts of interests underline the modern versions of the arguments raised against the 'universal banks' in the aftermath of the Great Depression. The US Glass-Steagall Act of 1933 imposed such a separation or a 'firewall' between the securities and commercial (retail) activities of banks. In the years that followed, some of the European countries also imposed similar restrictions to limit the emergence of universal banks. The repeal of the Glass-Steagall Act in 1999 and the initiatives in the EU in the 1980s and 1990s, most notably the Second Banking Directive (1989/646/EEC), have been the main drivers for the re-diversification of the banking models on both sides of the Atlantic.[2] As a result of these developments, the banks have turned increasingly to non-interest income sources and non-traditional activities.

Whilst diversification of individual banks might seem to reduce their overall risk and may be one of the central motives, there is also a systemic dimension to consider as this might make the system as a whole less diversified. Andy Haldane (2009) of the Bank of England suggests that as banks diversified into each others' traditional areas, and most especially into the capital markets business, the system became less diverse and, therefore, potentially more vulnerable to common shocks. Furthermore, the diversification of banks into derivatives trading also has a systemic dimension. Many commentators (and central bankers) argued before the crisis that credit-risk-shifting derivatives should make the system less risky because risks were spread more optimally. However, this seems not to have been the experience during the crisis. Rajan (1992) has suggested that these new instruments might have made the system less vulnerable in the face of small, uncorrelated shocks, but more vulnerable to large, correlated shocks.

The recent deregulation drive was supported by arguments to allow banks to achieve more favourable economies of scope and better diversification of risks (Barth et al., 2000).[3] The arguments were largely

---

[2] The diversified banking model reappeared in Europe prior to the Second Banking Directive of 1989. The Directive and the accompanying regulations have only harmonised the legal and regulatory framework applicable to all types of banks. In an attempt to enhance integration within the EU's internal market, the single banking passport was introduced, facilitating cross-border businesses and introducing common regulatory and supervisory standards. The regulations have nevertheless enhanced the expansion opportunities of EU banks, both geographically and in scope.

[3] The discussion on the separation of banks' activities resurfaced in the midst of the financial crisis in the US during the deliberations for the Dodd-Frank Wall Street Reform and Consumer Protection Act. The original proposal, endorsed by President Obama in January 2010, contained the so-called 'Volcker rule' which

backed by evidence that failed to show substantial differences in the quality of securities underwritten by the universal banks and specialised investment houses (Kroszner & Rajan, 1994; Puri, 1994).

How does the universal banking model fare in terms of risk-taking, performance and efficiency in the light of recent evidence? A number of empirical studies have addressed this question. The common finding is that although diversification may expand the range of opportunities, these benefits may be more than offset by the costs from increased exposure to volatility (DeYoung & Roland, 2001; Stiroh, 2004 and 2006b; Stiroh & Rumble, 2006). Focarelli et al. (2011) show that securities underwritten by universal banks are riskier than those underwritten by specialised investment houses. The authors, however, argue that the increased risk-taking is due to an attempt to expand market share, and not conflicts of interest. Others have found that although diversification may enhance market valuations, expanding banks hold much less capital and engage in more risky activities (Demsetz & Strahan, 1997; Baele et al., 2007; Demirgüç-Kunt & Huizinga, 2010b).

An important development in the banking sectors in most developing countries since the 1990s is the rapid growth of securitisation and structured products.[4] In a nutshell, securitisation allows banks to pool their risky assets and sell them to outside investors, potentially transferring the associated credit risks to the markets.[5] Traditionally, the growth in these transactions has been justified by the mutual benefits they offer to both investors and originators. From the point of view of the investors, buying the products has been attractive due to the diversification benefits – as long as the products are not correlated with other holdings. From the lender's perspective, the transaction eliminates exposure to risks and, in the case of regulated entities, reduces required capital charges.

---

would have prohibited banks from engaging in purely proprietary trading and put severe restrictions on owning or investing in hedge funds or private equity funds. A much watered-down version of the bill was enacted in June 2010, which allowed banks to engage in a broader range of proprietary trading activities.

[4] As argued in Duffee & Zhou (2001), among other structured products, credit default swaps can also be used for the purpose of transferring risks to other investors.

[5] See Neal (1996) for an early discussion on the use of structured products for controlling credit risk. See also Brunnermeier (2009, pp. 78-82) for a concise description of securitisation and other structured products.

The benign view of securitisation and structured products has been challenged during the 2007-09 financial crisis. To summarise, the rising popularity of these transactions have led to a "flood of cheap credit" and growth of an interconnected institutions that are not regulated, or 'shadow banks' (Brunnermeier, 2009; Pozsar et al., 2010). A particularly critical argument has been the effect of securitisation on credit standards. Since most credit risks are borne by outside investors, banks had little incentive to properly screen (and monitor) loans.[6] There is mounting empirical evidence that credit standards were indeed incrementally lowered in the US prior to the crisis (Mian & Sufi, 2009; Keys et al., 2010). There are also questions concerning the extent to which the originators were able to offload their risks. Although the SPVs are, at least in theory, legally separate entities, the originating institution nevertheless had substantial exposures from the liquidity enhancements and forms of retained interests (Gorton et al., 2006). Indeed, originating institutions have taken a substantial part of the losses during the crisis, achieving "securitisation without risk transfer" (Greenlaw et al., 2008; Shin, 2009; Acharya et al., 2010b). According to these arguments, structured products are attractive because they allowed the originating institutions to expand their balance sheets while reducing their capital charges, potentially facilitating regulatory arbitrage.[7]

A parallel development to the diversification of banking activities has been the diversification of funding strategies. Over the past few years, many banks have reduced their reliance on traditional retail depositors and turned to short-term funding in the interbank and wholesale markets. In essence, short-term funds allow banks to manage their balance sheet sizes actively in a highly pro-cyclical manner (Adrian & Shin, 2008 and 2010). In this manner, the diversification of funding strategies is an offshoot of the increasing trading activities. For banks that engage heavily in trading, when the value of mark-to-market securities increases, their equity also

---

[6] The concern that securitisation may lower credit standards is not new. Gorton & Pennacchi (1995) model a bank's choice between holding loans and selling them, focusing on the potential for moral hazard. They conclude that if the banks hold a certain fraction of the securitised loans (or provide limited recourse), then the moral hazard problem could be partly mitigated. See also Ayadi & Behr (2009) for a similar argument for the credit derivatives markets.

[7] See also Jones (2000) on the potential use of structured products and derivative transactions for achieving regulatory arbitrage.

increases. The institutions use this 'surplus capacity' to expand their balance sheets even further by borrowing and issuing new securities. Repurchase agreements (repos) and reverse repurchase agreements (reverse repos), in which a financial institution sells a security (or buys it, in the case a reverse repo) to buy (or sell) it back later, are extremely suitable for this purpose. Institutions may also expand their activities and borrowing through the use of off-balance sheet special purpose vehicles (Acharya et al., 2010b).

The literature provides divergent views on the impact of the increased use of these short-term funding (and lending) alternatives. The 'bright-side' argument suggests that relying more on market funding may enhance market discipline. Provided that they are credibly excluded from the safety net, holders of subordinated debt may perform monitoring roles that cannot be fulfilled by the small and dispersed depositor holders (Calomiris & Kahn, 1991; Calomiris, 1999). More pessimistically, however, the market's monitoring incentives could be undermined by the expectation of government intervention in the 'too-big-to fail' (TBTF) banks, i.e. moral hazard. When a bail-out is a credible likelihood, the market's perception of risk may diverge substantially from the stand-alone risk represented by the bank's operations. Apart from weakening the debt-holders' incentives to apply monitoring and market discipline, i.e. moral hazard, such imperfections may also motivate banks to become large enough to be considered too-big-to-fail.[8] There is some empirical evidence (also supported by this study) suggesting that banks that are judged to be TBTF receive a superior rating, other things being equal, which in turn lowers the cost of market funding.

Another argument against the heavy use of short-term funding is the potential drying-up of liquidity in the event of a crisis. When banks become reliant on short-term financing, such as overnight repos, they need to rollover a substantial part of their funding on a daily basis, making them severely exposed to a sudden drying up of liquidity. Short-term lending, such as reverse-repo transactions, also exposes institutions to liquidity risk, seriously undermining the value of any collateral backing the transaction. In short, the trend towards the increasing use of these short-term instruments was seen to be among the chief explanations for the

---

[8] Banks may also outgrow their optimal size and may overextend their activities if doing so allows the management to extract private benefits, such as more power or compensation or to build empires (Jensen & Meckling, 1976; Jensen, 1986).

cataclysmic setbacks faced by some banks in the early phases of the financial crisis (Brunnermeier, 2009; Adrian & Shin, 2010).

By and large, the literature has confirmed that state support is likely to dampen the risks of debt-holders (even if the bank is inherently risky), potentially giving rise to increased moral hazard. O'Hara & Shaw (1990) find evidence of net positive wealth effects accruing to large US banks covered by the partial deposit insurance schemes put in place in the mid-1980s. Kane (2000) and Benston et al. (1995) show that bank mergers and acquisitions in the same period were partly motivated by the aim of creating institutions that were large enough to be covered by the US deposit insurance system. In addition to the gains for shareholders, Penas & Unal (2004) find that bond-holders also stand to benefit from state support that is granted to too-big-to-fail institutions. Implicit government insurance effectively serves to weaken (if not reverse) the correlation between individual bank risk and debenture yields (Flannery & Sorescu, 1996). Moreover, the sensitivity of the subordinated note spreads to measures of stand-alone risk is lower for state-owned banks and during periods of fiscal ease, i.e. when government support is more credible (Sironi, 2003).[9]

The empirical literature has therefore provided ample support to the idea that the monitoring roles of debt-holders may be undermined when state intervention is judged to be likely. Moreover, owing to their ability to pull back from the markets relatively quickly, short-term creditors may also have fewer incentives to conduct proper monitoring (Huang & Ratnovski, 2010). This would offset one of the key arguments for supporting the diversification of the funding strategies. As the recent financial crisis amply demonstrated, an excessive reliance on market funding may also invite other risks, such as a sudden drying-up of liquidity. Even small changes in an institution's underlying value can lead to a 'catastrophic drop' in roll-over debt capacity and de-leveraging, much like the one that was observed in the early phases of the crisis (Acharya et al., 2010a; Acharya & Viswanathan, 2011). Recent evidence supports these arguments, showing that non-deposit wholesale funding increases bank fragility (Demirgüç-Kunt & Huizinga, 2010b).

---

[9] In a similar vein, Demirgüç-Kunt & Huizinga (2010a) provide evidence that during the 2007-09 financial crisis, large banks saw a deterioration of their market valuations and credit default swap spreads in countries with large public deficits.

To sum up, the economics literature has provided a number of reasons why banks seek to diversify their activities and funding strategies. However, diversification may in some cases undermine social welfare and financial stability, especially in the presence of informational rents, conflicts of interest and moral hazard risks. In view of the 2007-09 financial crisis, the recent literature singles out the excessive reliance on market-based funding as a potentially harmful practice. These concerns are particularly acute when market participants have little incentive to monitor the banks due to the implicit or explicit government guarantees enjoyed by the banks and their creditors.

4. DATA AND METHODOLOGY

4.1 Sample selection and data

The European banking sector incorporates a rich array of banks, with different business models and ownership structures. Apart from the larger commercial retail and investment (universal) banks, which focus on a broad mix of banking activities, a large number of specialised institutions with different ownership structures – public banks, cooperatives, and savings institutions – co-exist in this highly diversified market. To a large extent, the business models can be distinguished by the scope of activities and funding strategies they engage in. Most retail-oriented banks, such as commercial, savings and cooperative banks, provide traditional banking services to the general public.[10] Investment-oriented banks focus more on trading activities, relying on a variety of funding sources and often maintaining a retail network of their own. Other banks provide services to their institutional clients, including large and mid-sized corporations, real estate developers, international trade finance businesses, network institutions and other financial institutions.

The sample under study comprises 26 large banks and banking groups that are headquartered in the EU, accounting for nearly 55% of the

---

[10] Although most savings and cooperative institutions are local – leaving them outside the scope of this study – they nevertheless depend on the services of much larger central institutions, which typically provide their network institutions with liquidity and represent the group on a consolidated basis for supervisory purposes (Desrochers & Fischer, 2005). Recent empirical work has shown that the local institutions have comparable performance and efficiency characteristics to their commercial peers and have largely weathered the financial crisis unscathed. However, a number of Spanish savings banks and the German central institutions have been hit hard. For more discussion on the European cooperative and savings banks, see Ayadi et al. (2009 and 2010).

EU's banking assets.[11] The sample selection exercise aimed to choose the largest banks (as of 2009) in terms of size of banking activity, i.e. the total consolidated assets. The sample covers the years 2006 to 2009; data for 2010 were not available at the time of the collection exercise. This leads to 108 bank-year observations.

The list of the sampled banks, their ownership types, total assets and growth of assets for recent years are given in Table 4.1. To account for mergers that have taken place in recent years, all of the large pre- and post-merger entities that qualify as the largest banks have been included in the database. In particular, the list covers the French Caisse d'Epargne and Banque Populaire, which were merged in 2009 to form the BPCE Group, and the Italian Banca Intesa and Sanpaolo IMI, which merged in 2007 to form the Intesa Sanpaolo.

Following the determination of the sample, a database of a large variety of variables was compiled to get a picture of the business model, profitability, asset and liability structure, earnings performance, stability and governance aspects for each one of the sampled banks over the time period covered. The compilation exercise relied mostly on publicly available information obtained from the banks' annual reports and financial statements. Other variables summarising the public interventions were also collected, supplemented with information from major international journals and public sources, such as the European Commission's state aid approval documents.[12] In addition, data from a pre-existing database on executive compensation in the EU's largest banks, compiled by CEPS, were also used.[13] Lastly, the information on share prices and CDS spreads was obtained from Yahoo Finance and Fitch Solutions, respectively.

---

[11] With total assets of €23.3 trillion in 2009, the sample represents nearly 55% of the EU total banking assets (€42.1 trillion), using ECB (2010) aggregate figures. Country-by-country shares could not be calculated due to the consolidated figures used in the study.

[12] See http://ec.europa.eu/competition/elojade/isef/index.cfm?clear=1&policy_area_id=3 for the European Commission's database on state aid documents.

[13] See Ayadi, Arbak & de Groen (forthcoming) for research on executive compensation in EU's banking sector using a comparable sampling period and data.

Table 4.1 List of banks examined in the report

Rank (2009)	Name	Country	Type of ownership (as of year-end 2009)	Total assets (€ mil., 2009)	Change in assets (%, 2006-09)
1	BNP Paribas	FR	Commercial bank	2,057,698	42.9%
2	Royal Bank of Scotland	UK	Nationalised	1,910,242	94.7%
3	HSBC Holdings plc	UK	Commercial bank	1,641,297	27.1%
4	Crédit Agricole S.A.	FR	Cooperative bank	1,557,300	23.5%
5	Barclays PLC	UK	Commercial bank	1,552,673	38.3%
6	ING Group N.V.	NL	Commercial bank	1,164,000	-5.1%
7	Deutsche Bank AG	DE	Commercial bank	1,500,664	-5.3%
8	Lloyds Banking Group	UK	Commercial bank	1,156,688	199.0%
9	Banco Santander S.A.	ES	Commercial bank	1,110,529	33.2%
10	BPCE Group*	FR	Savings bank	1,028,800	..
11	Société Générale	FR	Commercial bank	1,023,700	7.0%
12	UniCredit Group	IT	Commercial bank	928,760	12.8%
13	Commerzbank Group	DE	Commercial bank	844,103	38.8%
..	Groupe Caisse d'Epargne*	FR	Savings bank	649,756***	..
14	Intesa Sanpaolo Group**	IT	Commercial bank	624,844	..
15	Rabobank Group	NL	Cooperative bank	607,698	9.2%
16	Dexia SA	BE	Commercial bank	577,630	1.9%
17	Banco Bilbao Vizcaya Argentaria	ES	Commercial bank	535,065	29.9%
18	Nordea Bank AB	SE	Commercial bank	507,544	46.3%
19	ABN Amro Holding N.V.	NL	Nationalised	469,345	-52.5%
20	Dankse Bank Group	DK	Commercial bank	416,361	13.1%
21	Landesbank Baden-Württemberg	DE	Savings bank	411,694	-1.3%
..	Banque Populaire Group*	FR	Cooperative bank	403,589***	..
22	DZ Bank AG	DE	Cooperative bank	388,525	-7.9%
23	Hypo Real Estate Holding AG	DE	Fully Nationalised	359,676	122.6%
24	Bayerische Landesbank	DE	Savings bank	338,818	-1.6%
25	KBC Group NV	BE	Commercial bank	324,231	-0.4%
..	Banca Intesa**	IT	Commercial bank	291,781****	..
..	Sanpaolo IMI**	IT	Commercial bank	288,551****	..
26	WestLB AG	DE	Savings bank	242,311	-15.1%

* BPCE was created on 31 July 2009 through the merger of Groupe Caisse D'Epargne and Banque Populaire Group.

** Intesa Sanpaolo Group was created on 1 January 2007 by the merger of Banca Intesa and Sanpaolo IMI.

*** Amount at 31 December 2008.

****Amount at 31 December 2006.

The data collection exercise spanned over 200 variables for each bank/year observation (see Appendix I for a complete list). Following the collection exercise, a subset of the variables was selected based on data availability and relevance. Whenever possible, preference was given to variables with the highest coverage ratio, or the share of non-missing observations. Indicators on the banks' general structure, financial position, riskiness, crisis measures and governance were constructed from this subset. The final set of indicators used in identifying and assessing the business models is given in Table 4.2.

Table 4.2. Description of indicators used in the report

Variable	Coverage	Mean	Std. dev.	Min	Max
STRUCTURE					
Number of branches (per bil. € of assets)	92%	4.725	4.569	0.007	18.414
Number of employees (per bil. € of assets)	98%	0.100	0.058	0.004	0.232
OWNERSHIP					
Cooperative bank (dummy var.)	100%	0.139	0.347	0.000	1.000
Savings bank (dummy var.)	100%	0.148	0.357	0.000	1.000
State-owned bank (dummy var.) [a]	100%	0.157	0.366	0.000	1.000
Private block owners (% owned) [b]	100%	0.217	0.311	0.000	1.000
Listed on stock exchange (dummy var.)	100%	0.722	0.450	0.000	1.000
FINANCIAL ACTIVITIES					
Total assets (% of GDP)	100%	0.785	0.590	0.070	2.347
Customer loans (% of assets)	96%	0.427	0.160	0.092	0.714
Customer deposits (% of assets)	96%	0.314	0.119	0.037	0.597
Loans to banks (% of assets)	100%	0.115	0.087	0.006	0.406
Loans to public authorities (% of assets)	28%	0.220	0.222	0.014	0.678
Domestic assets (% of assets) [c]	100%	0.658	0.258	0.041	1.000
Reverse repurchase agreements (% of assets)	89%	0.070	0.048	0.009	0.233
Repurchase agreements (repos) (% of assets)	92%	0.076	0.051	0.000	0.228
Liquid assets (% of deposits) [d]	100%	0.014	0.012	0.001	0.063
Trading assets (% of assets) [e]	96%	0.440	0.169	0.194	0.893
Total derivative exposure (% of assets) [f]	95%	0.250	0.200	0.034	1.107
FINANCIAL PERFORMANCE					
Net interest income (% of total income)	100%	0.753	1.837	-3.240	18.803
Commission & fee income (% of total income)	100%	0.290	0.457	-1.332	4.500
Trading income (% of total income)	98%	-0.113	2.354	-23.213	5.106
Return on assets (RoA) [g]	100%	0.004	0.006	-0.015	0.017
Return on equity (RoE) [g]	100%	0.081	0.252	-1.166	1.473
Cost-to-income ratio (CIR) [h]	100%	0.762	1.432	-3.180	14.664
RISK					
Z-score (no. of std. devs. from default) [i]	89%	17.395	28.695	-0.889	152.862
Risk-weighted assets (RWA) (% of assets)	87%	0.373	0.125	0.140	0.693
CDS spread (annual avg., basis points)	69%	61.239	49.249	4.442	223.715
Stock return volatility (std. dev. of daily returns)	67%	0.030	0.019	0.009	0.082
Tier 1 capital ratio (% of risk-weighted assets)	87%	0.085	0.024	0.034	0.199
Tangible common equity (% of assets) [j]	100%	0.025	0.010	0.002	0.055

CRISIS					
Government guarantees (dummy var.)	100%	0.259	0.440	0.000	1.000
Government recapitalisation (dummy var.)	100%	0.546	0.500	0.000	1.000
GOVERNANCE					
Total audit fees (per 000's of € of assets)	90%	0.032	0.013	0.006	0.063
Statutory audit fees (per 000's of € of assets)	87%	0.023	0.011	0.004	0.051
Long-term bonus plan (dummy var.)	89%	0.740	0.441	0.000	1.000
Formal option plan (dummy var.)	89%	0.646	0.481	0.000	1.000
Annual bonuses (% of total annual pay)	67%	0.347	0.304	0.000	0.876
Compensation committee (dummy var.)	89%	0.729	0.447	0.000	1.000

Notes:
[a] At least 50% owned by public authorities.
[b] Private block owners are those that own more than a 5% stake, excluding the stakes of domestic public authorities.
[c] Whenever data on domestic assets were unavailable in annual reports, aggregate data on assets of foreign affiliates were used.
[d] Liquid assets are cash and balances at the central bank divided by total deposits.
[e] Trading assets are total assets minus liquid assets (cash and deposits at central bank) minus total loans minus intangible assets.
[f] Total derivative exposures are the sum of positive and negative fair values of all derivative transactions.
[g] Before-tax profits are used to calculate both RoA and RoE figures.
[h] CIR is defined as the ratio of total operating expenses divided by total income.
[i] See Appendix II for details on the calculation of z-score.
[j] Tangible common equity is common equity minus intangible assets (goodwill and other) minus treasury shares; common equity is defined as common stock plus additional paid-in capital plus retained earnings.
[k] Long-term bonus plans are those that reward the CEOs with cash or shares, conditional on multiple-year performance criteria.
[l] Share of annual bonus (excluding long-term bonuses) in total annual pay.

4.2 Methodology

In line with the study's aim of identifying different business models and screening for major weaknesses, the analysis is conducted in two phases. In the first phase, several instruments from Table 4.2 were used as a basis for the creation of distinct business models with the use of cluster analysis tools. In the second phase, the business models were evaluated and compared based on their relative performance, riskiness, governance and other relevant factors.

Loosely defined, cluster analysis is a statistical technique for assigning a set of observations (i.e. a particular bank in a particular year) into distinct clusters (i.e. business models). By definition, observations that are assigned to the same cluster share a certain degree of similarity, measured by a set of instruments. The formation of clusters ensures that they are sufficiently dissimilar between themselves, identifying different distinguishing characteristics of the observations they represent. To create the clusters, the initial step, is to determine a set of instruments for identifying any similarities or distinctions. The second step – more technical in nature – is to determine the methods for measuring similarities, for partitioning the clusters, and for determining the appropriate number of clusters (i.e. the 'stopping rule').

One of the key problems often encountered in clustering is the presence of missing values. When a particular observation has one or more missing instrument values, it has to be dropped from the cluster analysis since the similarity measures cannot be computed. The sample used in the study contains many such cases, despite efforts to choose indicators with high coverage ratios. In order to accommodate the entire sample of observations in the cluster analysis, multiple imputation techniques were used to fill in missing values with OLS regression estimates using the existing set of indicators as predictors. Potential errors were accounted for by producing a total of 10 random estimates, drawn randomly from the predicted distributions.[14] This procedure multiplied the sample size by a factor of 10, comprising 10 datasets that are exact copies of one another except for the randomly drawn or filled-in estimates. The cluster analysis was applied to the pooled dataset, providing a confidence level for observations involving missing values.

Assuming that banks consciously choose their business models, any cluster analysis should be based on instruments over which the banks can have a direct influence. For example, a bank is likely to have a great degree of choice over its general structure, financial position and some of the risk indicators.[15] In turn, most of the performance indicators are related to instruments that are beyond the bank's control, such as market conditions, systemic risks, consumer demand, etc. This was indeed one of the principal reasons why details on income sources (i.e. interest vs. non-interest income) were not used as instruments in the creation of the clusters.

The business models used in the study distinguish between the key banking activities, funding strategies, financial exposures, risks and

---

[14] The use of a greater number of imputations (i.e. 20 or 30) did not change the results.

[15] All of the instruments used for clustering were standardised so that each indicator had a mean zero and a standard deviation of one. This was done to prevent any potential biases arising from the choice of units, i.e. use of percentages rather than basis points.

geographic orientation. To account for these factors collectively, without over-representing any particular factor, six instruments were used to form the clusters.[16] These were:

1. *Customer deposits (as % of assets).* The indicator identifies the share of deposits from non-bank and private customers, e.g. households or enterprises, in the total balance sheet, indicating reliance on more traditional funding sources.

2. *Trading assets (as % of assets).*[17] Defined as non-cash assets other than loans, a greater value would indicate the prevalence of investment activities that are prone to market and liquidity risks.

3. *Loans to banks (as % of assets).* The indicator measures the scale of wholesale and interbank activities, which proxy for exposures to risks arising from interconnectedness in the banking sector.

4. *Total derivative exposures (as % of assets).*[18] This measure aggregates all the positive and negative derivative exposures of a bank, which are often identified as one of the key (and most risky) financial exposures of banks with heavy investment and trading activities.

5. *Tangible common equity (as % of assets).*[19] The indicator focuses on the most loss-absorbing parts of a bank's capital structure, providing an insight into the bank's risk attitudes and its leverage.

6. *Domestic activity (as % of assets).*[20] While banks that are more domestically-oriented are likely to face less cross-border risks, they may also face more concentration risks.

---

[16] Alternative instrument combinations were also considered. In many cases, using a different set of instruments led to an unrealistically large number of clusters, with many comprising a single bank/year. Removing any one of the six indicators from the clustering exercise also led to an indistinct clustering. In turn, using a larger set did not change the results substantially, as long as the named indicators were included.

[17] Trading assets are defined as total assets minus liquid assets (cash and deposits at central bank) minus total loans minus intangible assets.

[18] Total derivative exposures are defined as the summation of positive and negative fair value of all derivative transactions, including interest, currency, equity, OTC, hedge and trading derivatives.

[19] Tangible common equity is defined as common equity minus intangible assets (goodwill and other) minus treasury shares; common equity is defined as the sum of common stocks, additional paid-in capital and retained earnings.

Turning to the technical aspects, Ward's (1963) procedures were used to form the clusters. The procedures form partitions in a hierarchical manner, starting from the largest number of clusters possible (i.e. all bank/years in a separate cluster) and merging clusters by minimising the within-cluster sum-of-squared-errors for any given number of clusters. Several studies found that the Ward clustering methods perform better than other clustering procedures for instruments that involve few outliers and in the presence of overlaps.[21] Moreover, to diagnose the appropriate number of clusters, the Calinski & Harabasz's (1974) pseudo-F index, i.e. the 'stopping rule', was used. The index is a sample estimate of the ratio of between-cluster variance to within-cluster variance.[22] The configuration with the greatest pseudo-F value was chosen as the most distinct clustering.

All of the multiple imputation and clustering procedures were conducted using Stata's built-in and user-contributed functions.[23]

It is important to highlight once again that cluster analysis is an inexact science. The assignment of individual banks to a specific cluster, or model, depends crucially on the choice of instruments and procedures, such as the proximity metric, procedures for forming clusters and the stopping rules used. Although the literature on the technical aspects of cluster analysis is relatively well-developed, there is little theory on why certain procedures perform better than others.[24] In choosing instruments, attention was given to testing a variety of alternative configurations. The six indicators mentioned above led to the most consistent and distinct clustering. Dropping or adding variables resulted in a substantial

---

[20] Data on domestic assets were obtained primarily from annual reports; whenever the data were unavailable, it was set to equal the total assets of the bank's foreign affiliates divided by its total (consolidated) assets.

[21] See Milligan (1981) and references therein for an assessment of different clustering methods.

[22] Evaluating a variety of cluster stopping rules, Milligan & Cooper (1985) single out the Calinski and Harabasz index as the best and most consistent rule, identifying the sought configurations correctly in over 90% of all cases in simulations.

[23] The user-contributed 'ice.ado' procedure was used to conduct the multiple imputations for missing values. For the clustering exercise, the built-in procedures under the cluster function were used.

[24] See Everitt et al. (2001) for a highly readable introduction to cluster analysis and some of the practical issues in the choice of technical procedures.

worsening of the statistical measures of distinct clustering, which suggests that the chosen set adequately identifies the main distinguishing characteristics of the sampled banks. As the discussion below makes clear, the characteristics of the business models that are identified by the cluster analysis are by and large in line with expectations. Despite these efforts, it is certainly true that the outcomes may change with other configurations. For these reasons, the results of the present analysis should be interpreted with care.

5. RESULTS

The following discussion gives the details of the outcomes of the two phases of analysis. The first subsection provides the results of the cluster formation. The second subsection assesses the identified business models, based on a number of indicators of the banks' general structure, performance, riskiness, governance and other relevant factors.

5.1 Identification of business models

The clustering procedures summarised in the previous chapter lead to highly consistent results. In particular, the results show that the pseudo-F indices attain a single maximum, pointing to the three-cluster configuration as the most distinct one (see Table 5.1).

Table 5.1 Pseudo-F indices for clustering configurations

Number of clusters	Pseudo-F index (Calinski & Harabasz)	Number of clusters	Pseudo-F index (Calinski & Harabasz)
2	401.9	9	363.8
3	**473.0**	10	372.4
4	398.2	11	362.6
5	376.9	12	356.8
6	364.7	13	354.7
7	356.7	14	353.4
8	361.3	15	352.2

Note: The Calinski & Harabasz's (1974) pseudo-F index is an estimate of the between-cluster variance divided by within-cluster variance.

The descriptive details for the three clusters are given below in Table 5.2 and Figure 5.1. Keeping in mind the word of caution noted at the end of the previous chapter, the three business models can be characterised as follows.

Model 1, or the so-called 'retail' banks model, comprises 40 bank/year observations. In essence, these banks use customer deposits as the primary means for funding and maintain a relatively high level of loss-absorbing capital. The cluster mean for the share of customer deposits in the balance sheet total is nearly 42%, which is almost one standard deviation greater than the sample average and the sub-sample averages (and the maxima) for the two other models. In turn, the cluster average for the tangible common equity to total assets ratio is 3.1%, which is greater than the averages of the other models. In line with their identification as retail banks, these banks are less likely to engage in trading activities, with non-cash and non-loan assets accounting for one-third of the total assets on average, which is lower than the sample mean and the averages for other clusters.

Table 5.2 Descriptive statistics for three clusters

		Customer deposits (% of assets)	Trading assets (% of assets)	Loans to banks (% of assets)	Derivative exposures (% of assets)	Tangible common equity (% of assets)	Domestic assets (% of assets)
Model 1 - Retail banks (40 obs.)	Mean	42.2% **	32.9% **	8.0% **	15.6% **	3.1% **	53.4% **
	Std. dev.	0.066	0.091	0.032	0.086	0.007	0.271
	Min.	0.303	0.194	0.033	0.034	0.014	0.041
	Max.	0.597	0.554	0.171	0.398	0.052	0.998
Model 2 - Investment banks (24 obs.)	Mean	23.0% *	64.7% **	4.6% **	51.1% **	1.9% **	58.2% **
	Std. dev.	0.073	0.125	0.029	0.236	0.007	0.176
	Min.	0.087	0.419	0.006	0.245	0.010	0.350
	Max.	0.362	0.893	0.127	1.107	0.035	0.918
Model 3 - Wholesale banks (44 obs.)	Mean	23.8% *	43.8% **	19.4% **	18.5% **	2.3% **	83.8% **
	Std. dev.	0.083	0.133	0.089	0.095	0.010	0.160
	Min.	0.037	0.278	0.082	0.074	0.002	0.404
	Max.	0.382	0.713	0.406	0.494	0.055	1.000
All banks (108 obs.)	Mean	31.4%	44.0%	11.5%	25.0%	2.5%	65.8%
	Std. dev.	0.119	0.168	0.087	0.200	0.010	0.256
	Min.	0.037	0.194	0.006	0.034	0.002	0.041
	Max.	0.597	0.893	0.406	1.107	0.055	1.000

Note: The independence of cluster sub-samples was tested using the Wilcoxon-Mann-Whitney non-parametric two-sample tests at 5% significance. According to these tests, a single asterisk (*) signifies statistical difference from a single cluster, i.e. the furthermost cluster; two asterisks (**) signify statistical difference from both clusters.

Figure 5.1 Comparison of cluster means, standardised* scores

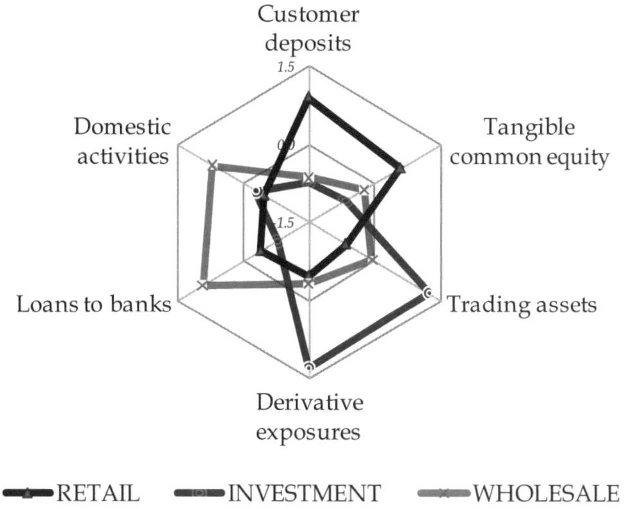

* The figures represent the number of standard deviations from the sample mean, implying that any observation above (below) the zero-axis is above (below) the sample mean.

Model 2, or the 'investment' banks model, comprises 24 bank/year observations. As its name clearly implies, the cluster groups together banks that have a tendency to engage predominantly in investment activities. In particular, the cluster average for trading assets and derivative exposures are more than one standard deviation above the sample mean and the minima for these two instruments are above the averages of other clusters. In turn, these banks are much less likely to engage in interbank lending and are substantially more leveraged, with an average tangible common equity-to-total-assets ratio of barely 1%. Moreover, funding is obtained from more non-traditional sources with customer deposits representing less than one-quarter of the balance-sheet total.

Model 3, or the 'wholesale' banks model, is the largest group, comprising 44 observations. The banks in this group tend to be more domestically-oriented than the banks in other clusters. The cluster groups together banks that are heavily wholesale-oriented and active in the interbank markets. Indeed, interbank loans represent nearly one-fifth of the balance sheet totals of these banks, exceeding even the maxima for the other two clusters, i.e. 17.1% and 12.7% for retail and investment bank clusters, respectively. Moreover, much like investment banks, the share of customer deposits in total liabilities is lower than average, hinting at an extensive reliance on wholesale markets for funding sources.

Table 5.3 Assignment of banks to business models

Model 1 Retail Banks	Model 2 Investment Banks	Model 3 Wholesale Banks
ABN Amro (2006-07)	ABN Amro (2008)	ABN Amro (2009)
Banca Intesa (2006)	Barclays	Banque Populaire (2006-08)
Banco Bilbao	BNP Paribas	Bayerische Landesbank
Banco Santander	Commerzbank (2009)	BPCE Group (2009)
HSBC	Deutsche Bank	Commerzbank (2006-08)
ING	RBS (2008-09)	Crédit Agricole
Intesa Sanpaolo (2007-09)	Société Générale	Danske Bank Group
KBC	WestLB	Dexia
Lloyds		DZ Bank
Nordea		Groupe Caisse d'Epargne (2006-08)
Rabobank		Hypo Real Estate
RBS (2006)		Landesbank Baden-Württemberg
Sanpaolo IMI (2006)		RBS (2007)
UniCredit		

Notes: Due to the presence of missing data, there is a potential for mistaken assignments. To control for these errors, 10 values were drawn from predicted distributions generated for each missing value using multiple imputation techniques, leading to 10 data points for each bank/year observation (see previous chapter for details). According to the results of the cluster analysis, all of the data points for a given observation were assigned to the same model, implying a 95% confidence level.

Having characterised the three business models with which to study the 26 banks in the sample, Table 5.3 lists the banks according to the cluster(s) into which they fall. As the table clearly shows, although many banks have been assigned to a single cluster for the entire sample period, some banks have changed their models through the sampled period of 2006-09. For example, according to the cluster assignments, ABN-Amro has switched its business model twice in recent years. First, it switched from a retail bank model to an investment bank model in 2008, immediately after its takeover by the (former) Fortis, RBS and Banco Santander. And in 2009, the bank switched to the wholesale model, following its nationalisation by the Dutch government. RBS also started off as a retail bank in 2006, but appears to have switched to the investment banking model in 2008.

Figure 5.2 Transitions from one model to another

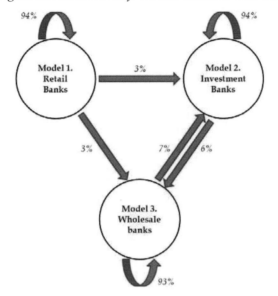

Note: The figures give the share of banks that belong to a specific model in one period switching to another model (or remaining assigned to the same model) in the next period.

Despite the occurrences of model switching, most banks are assigned to the same business model in the sampling period. Indeed, the transition probabilities depicted in Figure 5.2 show that the likelihood of being assigned to the same business model is greater than 90% in all three groups. Another result that emerges from the transition probabilities is that no bank has changed its orientation to become a retail bank. This stands in stark contrast with the ambitions stated by the management of some of the EU's top banks. In the years 2008-10, several banks that received state support have negotiated restructuring plans with the European Commission to concentrate on providing banking services to retail customers and small- and medium-sized firms and withdrawing from other 'non-core' activities.[25] Although our sample does not cover more

[25] The sampled banks that have negotiated a restructuring plan with the European Commission to concentrate more on retail activities include – with the Commission's approval dates cited in parentheses – Dexia (February 2010), KBC Group (November 2009), Commerzbank (May 2009), Landesbank Baden-Württemberg (December 2009), ING Group (November 2009), Lloyds (November 2009) and RBS (December 2009). Among these banks, the cluster analysis has

recent years, it does not show that such a transition occurred for any of the surveyed banks in 2008-09.

It is important to highlight once again that although the methods utilised in the study are chosen to limit the subjectivity in the procedures, the choice of instruments and procedures nevertheless play an important role in the identification of clusters and assignments of banks to a cluster. Certain banks may be more appropriately placed in distinctly different business models, engaging in a wider array of activities, which may extend well beyond the six instruments used here. It may also be more appropriate to focus more on certain activities than others in associating banks with a specific business model. The identification and assignment procedures take account of the average characteristics of each cluster, treating all the six covered instruments equally and disregarding others. For these reasons, the cluster names and the assignment of banks to individual clusters as depicted above should be interpreted with caution.

5.2   Assessment of models

To provide an overview of the evaluation of the different banking models in the discussion that follows, several key points can be highlighted. First, the results show that the performance and risk attributes vary considerably both over time and across different models. The retail banks, mostly comprising commercial banks relying on interest income, have continued to support the economy despite the crisis, thanks to their consistent performance. These banks appear to have taken fewer risks, performed comparably or even better than their peers, with slightly better governance practices than their peers. Wholesale banks tend to be more domestically-oriented and have an ownership structure that reflects stakeholder values (i.e. cooperative or savings banks). These banks perform worse than their peers and appear to be more risky, at least within the sampled period. Indeed, more than three-quarters of the wholesale banks received some form of state support in 2008-09, which is more than in any other group. Investment banks, which are also commercially-oriented, are somewhere in between, with significantly worsening performances during the crisis and a quick rebound in 2009.

---

placed Dexia, Commerzbank, Landesbank Baden-Württemberg and RBS outside the retail banking model. For more information and a bank-by-bank analysis of the state aid cases, see Appendix III.

Our results also show that despite these marked differences, market-based indicators of risk, such as CDS spreads, do not seem to reveal any disparities in riskiness of different banking models. Moreover, there does not appear to be a coherent link between risk measures derived from banks' financial statements and the risk-weights they apply to their activities, calling into question the effectiveness of risk-adjusted capital requirements. A deeper analysis of risk-taking in individual banks is made difficult by a number of factors, including most notably a general lack of data and opaqueness on banks' key risk exposures.

5.2.1 General structure and activities

The general structural attributes of the three business models are summarised in Table 5.4. The figures show that retail banks are clearly more customer-oriented, maintaining a more extensive network of branches and with more employees. In turn, investment banks and wholesale banks are smaller in size and are more capital-intensive. These observations are most likely the direct consequence of the relative size of the retail and non-retail activities of the banks. Banks with more retail activity need to be present in a broader geographical area, requiring a greater number of branches and a larger staff to engage directly with their retail customers. In turn, non-core trading and wholesale activities require less presence and a greater focus on trading systems and platforms.

Table 5.4 Structural attributes of business models

Attribute	Retail	Investment	Wholesale	All
Size (% of GDP)	95.2% **	72.6% **	63.6% **	78.5%
Branches (per bil. € of assets)	8.5 **	2.5 **	2.8 **	4.7
Employees (per bil. € of assets)	144.3 **	81.1 **	60.4 **	99.8

Notes: All figures are the mean values for the year-end observations for the relevant sample. The independence of cluster sub-samples was tested using the Wilcoxon-Mann-Whitney non-parametric two-sample tests at 5% significance. According to these tests, a single asterisk (*) signifies statistical difference from a single cluster, i.e. the furthermost cluster; two asterisks (**) signify statistical difference from both clusters.

The financial activities of the banks are also in line with their business models. Indeed, Table 5.5 shows that retail banks are more likely to provide customer loans, which represent more than half of their balance sheets. These banks have also maintained a high ratio of liquid assets, comprising cash and balances at the central bank. Although data availability is an issue, wholesale banks appear to devote approximately one-third of their balance sheets to lending to public authorities.[26] Their liquidity ratios are the lowest among the three models, implying potential risks. Investment banks, on the other hand, are less likely to provide loans, which is an extension of their strategy to engage in trading activities.

Table 5.5 Financial activities in business models

	Retail	Investment	Wholesale	All
Customer loans (% of assets)	55.4% **	28.6% **	36.5% **	42.7%
Loans to public authorities (% of assets)	1.7% **	5.0% **	34.0% **	22.0%
Reverse repurchase agreements (% of assets)	5.4% **	10.3% **	6.5% **	7.0%
Repurchase agreements (repos) (% of assets)	5.9% **	10.7% **	7.4% **	7.6%
Liquid assets (% of deposits)a	1.7% **	1.3% **	1.1% **	1.4%

Notes: All figures are the mean values for the year-end observations for the relevant sample. The independence of cluster subsamples was tested using the Wilcoxon-Mann-Whitney non-parametric two-sample tests at the 5% level of significance. According to these tests, a single asterisk (*) signifies statistical difference from a single cluster, i.e. the furthermost cluster; two asterisks (**) signify statistical difference from both clusters.

a Liquid assets are cash and balances at the central bank divided by total deposits.

Another interesting characteristic distinguishing the three business models is the differing use of short-term market transactions through the use of reverse repurchase agreements (reverse repos) and repurchase agreements (repos). Recent empirical work reveals that institutions with large trading portfolios often use these tools to adjust their fluctuating leverage levels by heavily engaging in these transactions, (Adrian & Shin, 2008 and 2010).[27] Indeed, reverse repo and repos accounted for nearly 10%

---

[26] Data on loans to public authorities were available for only 45% of the wholesale banks. Despite these shortcomings, there is reason to believe that these banks are substantially more likely to engage in these activities. In particular, the sample minimum for public loans was 14% for wholesale banks, which by and large exceeds the sample maxima for the retail and investment banks.

[27] The transactions are popular because they are collateralised, often by securitised bonds. In a typical repurchase agreement, the borrower sells some securities – often below the market price – only to buy them back at a later date and at a pre-

of the balance sheets of the investment banks in the sample period, which tend to have substantial trading activities. More generally, Figure 5.3 confirms the presence of a positive relationship between the size of trading book and its use of repo funding in our sample. To a large extent, investment banks, which tend to have very large trading assets, are more likely to use these transactions than others. Retail banks, on the other hand, are less active in the short-term funding markets, and evidently more reliant on deposits.

Figure 5.3 Relationship between trading activities and repo funding

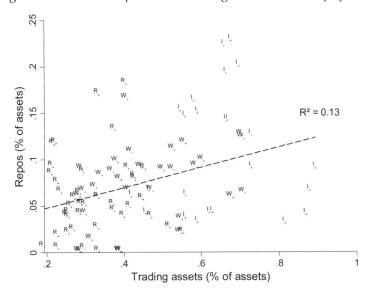

Note: The letters R, I and W stand for the retail, investment and wholesale banking models.

The evolution of repo funding throughout the crisis is of particular interest due to the worsening funding conditions. Starting from the early phases of the crisis, the repo market came under enormous pressure due to fears of counterparty default and declining security prices, especially for

---

set price. In turn, in a reverse repurchase agreement, the roles are reversed: the lender buys securities to sell them back at a pre-determined price at a later date. In either case, the security serves as collateral if the exchange does not take place under the agreed conditions. As noted in the literature review section, these transactions may expose the institutions to severe risks from a sudden drying up of liquidity in the markets, as was clearly shown in the early phases of the crisis.

structured products. Indeed, empirical research suggests that these conditions have led to a 'run on repos' in the US and Europe, first in August 2007 and later on in September 2008, in the aftermath of the failure of Lehman Brothers (Gorton & Metrick, forthcoming). Confirming these findings, Figure 5.4 shows that all business models reduced their use of repos substantially between 2006 and 2009. The greatest one-time drop, however, was for investment banks, whose use of repos dropped by more than one-third in the early phases of the crisis between 2007 and 2008.

Figure 5.4 Evolution of repo funding during crisis

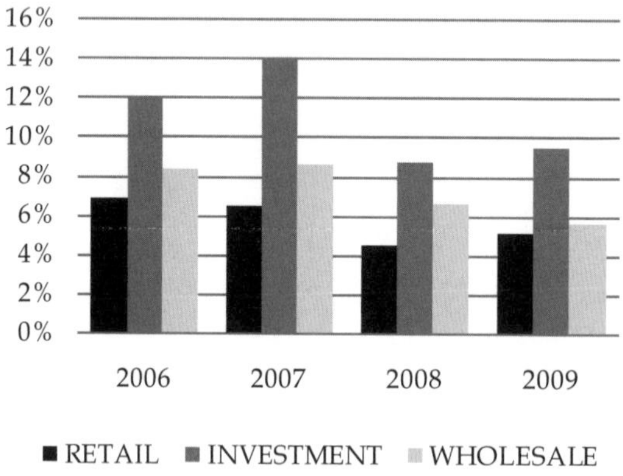

■ RETAIL ■ INVESTMENT ▪ WHOLESALE

Note: All figures are the mean values for the year-end observations for the relevant sample.

An important question to ask at this moment is whether the sampled banks within each business model have continued to support the economy by providing loans. There are many reasons to expect banks to change their lending strategies during a crisis. First, faced with losses and severe drops in asset prices, a troubled bank has two options to meet its regulatory requirements: it can either raise more capital – a costly option in bad times – or, more likely, shrink its assets.[28] Second, uncertainties about borrowers,

---

[28] When a bank chooses to issue capital, this may signal that the stock may be overvalued, which leads to a negative stock response and higher capital costs, (Myers & Majluf, 1984). Moreover, once a bank is in trouble and its debt is impaired in value, it may be reluctant to raise new equity, even for projects that are highly profitable, since part of the value created by the investment will be claimed by the creditors and not the shareholders (Myers, 1977). Given this so-called 'debt-overhang' problem, managers acting in line with the interests of the shareholders will tend to shrink assets rather than raise new equity.

especially in the interbank market when systemic risks exist, may lead to a reduction of lending, i.e. 'flight to quality' (Lang & Nakamura, 1995; Bernanke et al., 1996). A third reason to suspect changing credit issuance is the increasing risks associated with trading activities. The potential for downward swings may lead some institutions, mainly investment banks, to change their business strategies, reduce trading and issue loans to a safer class of customers. Finally, ultimately, whether one or more of these effects dominate depends largely on the underlying risks for the banks in question, the depth of the crisis, systemic risks and, more generally, market conditions.

Figure 5.5 shows that the growth in customer loans has declined substantially for investment and wholesale banks. The fact that the growth in customer loan portfolios of investment banks has slowed down hints at the possibility that some of these banks may be re-orienting their business towards retail lending. For wholesale banks, on the other hand, outstanding loans have dropped in 2009. Lastly, retail banks have continued to expand their lending despite the crisis, even at a faster pace in 2009 than in prior years. As will be explored in detail below, one possibility is that these banks have not been subject to the extent of losses faced by other categories and, thus, did not have to adjust balance sheets.

Figure 5.5 Change in outstanding customer loans from previous year

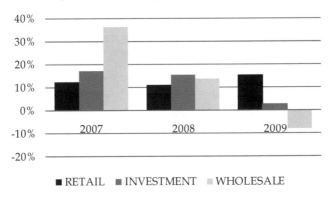

Note: All figures are the mean values for the year-end observations for the relevant sample.

The results confirm the expected characteristics of each business model. Retail banks engage more in customer loans, possibly aided by their extensive network of branches to undertake relationship banking. Investment banks, which by definition focus on trading activities, use short-term collateralised borrowing and lending transactions such as repos and reverse repos to actively manage their balance sheets. The findings also show that the use of these transactions have declined during the crisis, implying underlying difficulties. Despite these issues, both retail banks and investment banks have continued to increase their lending activities during the crisis. The same is not true for wholesale banks, which substantially shrank their lending.

5.2.2 *Performance*

Arguably one of the simplest means to distinguish banks' business models is to analyse their income characteristics, discriminating between interest income and other sources, such as commission income, fees and earnings from trading activities. Indeed, much of the literature depended on banks' income characteristics to distinguish them from one another.[29] Despite the ease with which such an analysis can be conducted in good times (i.e. income-related indicators are widely available), earnings fluctuate substantially during crises, leading to potentially erroneous assignments of banks to groups.

Figure 5.6 summarises the evolution of the income sources over the sampled period. The pre-crisis figures for 2006 show that the business models can clearly be distinguished with the use of these indicators. Retail banks and wholesale banks earn nearly half of their net income through interest-related products. For investment banks, however, trading income is the main driver, also representing half of net incomes on average. Commission and fee income is a secondary earnings source for all banks, corresponding to one-quarter of the total.

Although an earlier phase of the crisis, the 2007 figures show a substantial change in the earnings profiles for the investment and wholesale banks. Both have experienced a substantial drop in returns from trading activities. In particular, investment banks have ended the year with losses on their trading activities while wholesale banks have made essentially zero returns. In line with these developments, the share of other non-trading income streams has increased. Most notably, the share of interest income, assumed to be a relatively stable source of income, has increased for investment and wholesale banks, even surpassing that for retail banks.

---

[29] For the use of income characteristics to identify banks' underlying business models, see Stiroh (2004 and 2006a) and the references therein.

Figure 5.6 Evolution of main income sources during crisis

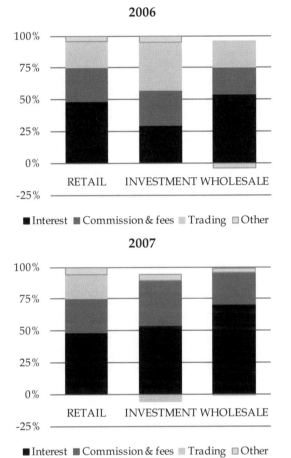

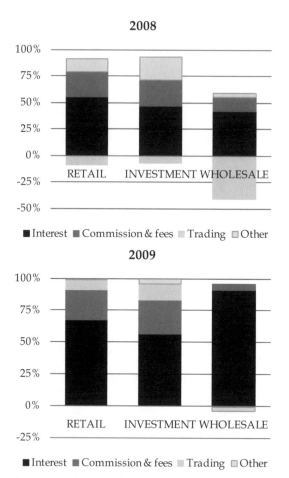

Note: All figures are the mean values for the year-end observations for the relevant sample.

In 2008, all three categories finished the year with trading losses. This is perhaps most evident for wholesale banks, which made substantial losses. Retail banks continue to depend mostly on their income earnings while a non-trivial proportion of the net income of investment banks is from non-traditional sources, including most notably insurance premium income. The year 2009 closes off with improving results for retail and investment banks, although interest sources have become the key income source for all banks. In particular, trading gains appear on the income statements of both retail and investment banks. Wholesale banks, however, make almost no non-interest income, which highlights a severe problem underlying their conditions.

Table 5.6 Performance of business models

	Retail		Investment		Wholesale		All
Return on assets (RoA)	0.73%	**	0.18%	**	0.08%	**	0.37%
Return on equity (RoE)	14.56%	**	5.45%	**	-1.09%	**	8.11%
Cost-to-income ratio (CIR)	59.19%	**	76.16%	*	94.92%	*	76.19%

Notes: All figures are the mean values for the year-end observations for the relevant sample. For the calculation of return on equity (RoE), observations with negative equity values were eliminated. The independence of cluster sub-samples was tested using the Wilcoxon-Mann-Whitney non-parametric two-sample tests at the 5% level of significance. According to these tests, a single asterisk (*) signifies statistical difference from a single cluster, i.e. the furthermost cluster; two asterisks (**) signify statistical difference from both clusters.

Figure 5.7 Evolution of earnings performance during the crisis

a) Return on assets (RoA)

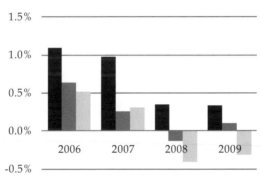

b) Return on equity (RoE)

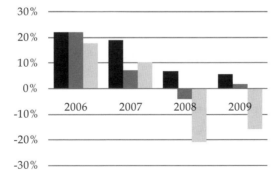

Notes: All figures are the mean values for the year-end observations for the relevant sample. For the calculation of return on equity (RoE), observations with negative equity values were eliminated. Both figures consider pre-tax profits, dividing them by assets (RoA) or equity (RoE).

The comparative performances of the three business models, summarised in Table 5.6 and Figure 5.7, confirm the strengths and weaknesses identified above. It is easy to see that the crisis has impacted the earnings of all banks, notwithstanding their business models. Even the average retail bank, which succeeded in remaining profitable despite the crisis, saw its earnings drop by more than two-thirds. However, the crisis had an uneven impact on the three business models. Due to their heavy trading losses in 2008, the wholesale banks obtained the worst profitability results, which have only been made worse by their negative return-on-equity (RoE) and return-on-asset (RoA) in the years 2008 and 2009. Investment banks also suffered, with negative average returns in 2008 and almost zero (pre-tax) profits in 2009. However, their earnings conditions bounced back in 2009, putting them back into profitability.

As another measure of performance, Table 5.6 provides the average cost efficiency of the three business models, as measured by the cost-to-income ratio (CIR). According to these results, retail banks have obtained the best results, with a CIR of under 60%, which is substantially lower than the sample mean and the averages for the two other models. The wholesale and investment banks are statistically indistinguishable on this aspect, despite a sizeable difference in the average values.

To sum up, the pre-crisis results on income sources confirm the expected characteristics of different business models. Much like in the rest of the literature, interest income is a predominant source of income for retail banks. Moreover, although the main contributor to the earnings of investment banks was trading income prior to the crisis, the fluctuating market conditions have made such a characterisation difficult. Wholesale banks clearly suffered substantially, mostly due to heavy trading losses in 2008. This has positioned them substantially behind the earnings performance of their rivals. Put together with their superior cost-efficiency performances, retail banks have clearly out-performed their peers, despite lowered earnings, during the crisis.

5.2.3 Risks

Table 5.7 Risks of business models

	Retail	Investment	Wholesale	All
Z-score (std. dev. from default) [a]	31.123 **	9.645 **	6.808 **	17.395
Risk-weighted assets (RWA) (% of assets)	46.5% **	28.3% **	31.3% **	37.3%
CDS spread (annual avg., basis points)	61.147	61.253	61.402	61.239
Stock returns volatility (std. dev. of daily returns)	2.8% *	3.6% **	2.9% *	3.0%
Tier 1 capital ratio (% of risk-weighted assets)	8.3% *	8.7% **	8.5% *	8.5%
Government support (guarantees or recap.)	43.2% **	66.7% **	80.0% **	62.0%

Notes: All figures are the mean values for the year-end observations (unless otherwise noted) for the relevant sample. The independence of cluster sub-samples was tested using the Wilcoxon-Mann-Whitney non-parametric two-sample tests at the 5% level of significance. According to these tests, a single asterisk (*) signifies statistical difference from a single cluster, i.e. the furthermost cluster; two asterisks (**) signify statistical difference from both clusters.

[a] See Appendix II for calculation of z-score.

We now turn to identifying the risks associated with the three business models. Table 5.7 provides the mean risk indicators for the three business models during the sampled period. Retail banks appear to be safer – but not in all measures. In particular, retail banks appear to be placed furthest from a potential default, i.e. low default likelihood, as evidenced by a high Z-score.[30] The retail banks' stock returns exhibit a low degree of volatility, statistically distinguishable from investment banks. Moreover, these banks were much less likely to receive government support, in the form of either liability guarantees or re-capitalisation/injection. In contrast, wholesale banks have the highest risks, with the lowest Z-scores – or highest default risks – among all models, which is backed by the amount of government support they received during the crisis.[31] When it comes to

---

[30] Since Z-scores are determined by the average and standard deviation of banks' return-on-assets, the only part that changes over time is the ratio of equity over assets, or simply the capital ratio.

[31] The wholesale banks included in the sample consist mostly of the large, central

market measures, especially the average CDS spreads, the three models are less distinguishable, implying that the markets have not picked a particular model for its riskiness over the sampling period.

How effective is the Z-score in measuring default likelihood? A look into the relationship between Z-score and government recapitalisation could be illuminating in assessing the indicator's accuracy in measuring distress.[32] In many cases, the authorities consider recapitalisation for banks that are facing financial difficulties, with a high likelihood of insolvency in the event of no intervention. This should mean that banks that receive no recapitalisation should be substantially safer (i.e. less likely to fail) than others. For other banks, Z-scores should be the lowest (pointing at a greater likelihood of default) in the year that recapitalisation is executed.

Figure 5.8 Evolution of Z-score before, during and after recapitalisation

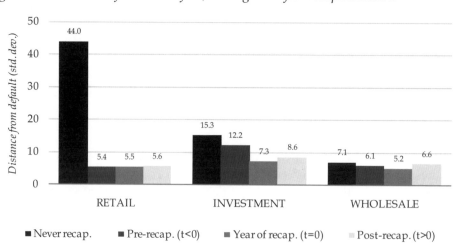

Notes: Post- and pre-capitalisation periods exclude the year of recapitalisation, i.e. the year in which the capital was provided. Where multiple recapitalisations were made, the year of initial transaction was considered.

---

institutions that provide liquidity and other functions for their cooperative and savings bank networks. Several studies have found that the smaller, retail cooperative and savings banks, which are not included in this study, have lower riskiness than their commercial peers in Europe (Čihák & Hesse, 2007; Ayadi et al., 2009 and 2010).

[32] A similar look into government guarantees was not possible since the exact dates for which guarantees were provided were not available in some cases.

Figure 5.8 shows that banks that are never recapitalised are indeed much safer, with a high Z-score. This is particularly striking for the retail banks, whose default likelihoods are among the lowest in our sample. Moreover, for investment and wholesale banks that did receive recapitalisation, the default likelihoods behave exactly in the way hypothesised above. Indeed, Z-scores decline to an all-time low in the year that recapitalisation is made, implying greater default likelihoods, which most likely triggered the intervention. The conditions improve in the years following the recapitalisation. These results confirm that the Z-scores serve well as a measure of potential default likelihood, at least in our sample.[33]

As for other risk measures, retail banks appear to have the highest risk-weights (i.e. risk-weighted assets, or RWA), as a share of total assets, presented in Figure 5.9a among the three business models, implying that the regulatory measure of their risks is higher. Figure 5.9b shows a lower Tier-1 capital ratio for retail banks, which implies that their loss absorption capacity (as defined by Tier-1 capital) is smaller than their peers, especially the investment banks which have statistically distinguishable ratios. The Tier-1 ratios have also improved over time, as banks had to increase their capital in line with the market expectations and, in some cases, due to the regulators' insistence, especially in the case of banks that received government support and following the first stress test held by the Committee of European Banking Supervisors (CEBS), or the European Banking Authority (EBA) under its new name, in July 2010.

---

[33] Interestingly enough, the results are not found to be purely driven by the changing capital conditions. Indeed, in many cases, banks that were never recapitalised appear to also hold less capital (as a share of assets, risk-weighted assets, etc.) than their peers. This implies that other components of the Z-score contribute to explaining a substantial part of our results. For example, banks with low capital may be deemed safe if their earnings volatility is low and/or their mean earnings are high.

Figure 5.9 Evolution of regulatory indicators during crisis

a) Risk-weighted assets (RWA)

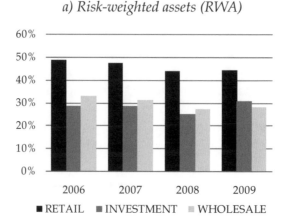

b) Tier-1 capital ratio

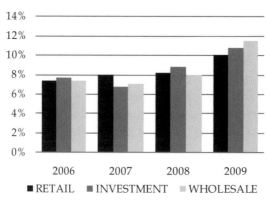

Note: Risk-weighted assets are expressed as a percentage of total assets and Tier-1 capital ratio as a percentage of risk-weighted assets.

So how can these seemingly conflicting results be reconciled? The differing results on Z-score, risk-weights and the CDS spreads merit deeper investigation. One way to explain these distinctions is that market measures tend to consider actual outcomes; the Z-score, on the other hand, measures inherent risks, which may not materialise if, say, the government steps in to bail out the banks. Indeed, the fact that CDS spreads are statistically indistinguishable for all banks seems to confirm that these dynamics are really at play.

Figure 5.10 depicts the evolution of stock return volatility (a) and CDS spreads throughout the crisis (b). Both measures point at increased risks, starting essentially from 2008. However, the figures show that the market has associated each model with more or less similar risks. This is particularly striking in the CDS spreads where all three models are associated with statistically indistinguishable risks. Therefore, it is likely that the market has already factored in the likelihood that no matter how risky they may inherently be, the EU's top banks will be bailed out, possibly resulting in comparable risks for all institutions. These findings thus give support to the arguments on the elevation of moral hazard risks arising from missing or diluted market discipline in the presence of bank bail-outs, (Calomiris & Kahn, 1991; Rochet & Tirole, 1996; Diamond & Rajan, 2001).

Figure 5.10 Evolution of market risk measures during crisis

a) Stock return volatility

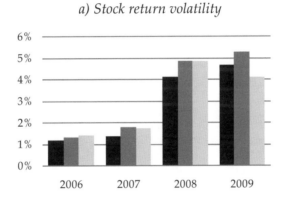

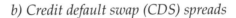

b) Credit default swap (CDS) spreads

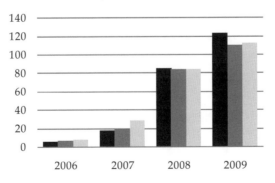

Notes: Stock return volatility in a) are expressed in standard deviations in stock returns, calculated by using daily closing prices. Credit Default Swap (CDS) spreads in b) are expressed in average annual spreads, in basis points.

Figure 5.11 Relationship between Z-score and RWA

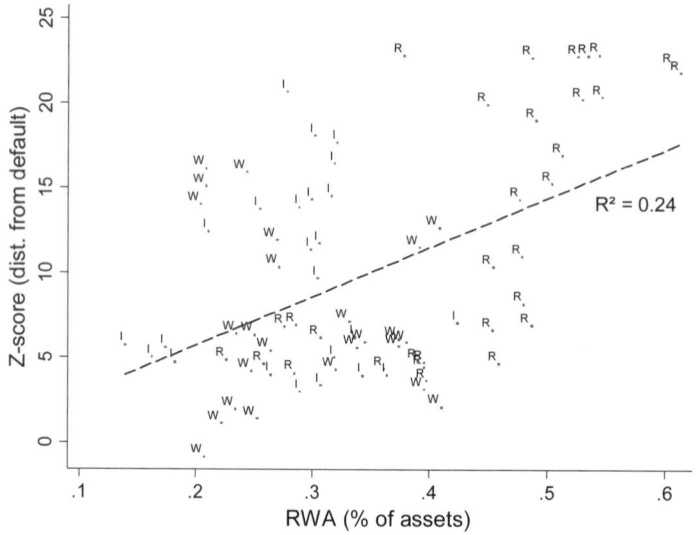

Notes: The letters R, I and W stand for the retail, investment and wholesale banking models. See Appendix II for details on the calculation of the Z-score. The coefficient estimate for RWA is significant at the 1% level.

The conflict between the default risks as measured by the Z-score and the mean risk-weights is less easy to explain. Figure 5.11 shows a strong positive correlation between the two measures. Contrary to what one would expect, the diagram suggests that as the bank's risk-weighted assets increase, implying a higher regulatory measure of risk, Z-score improves, implying a *lower* default likelihood. Why should banks with higher average risk-weights have much lower likelihood of default?

One potential explanation of the interesting result in Figure 5.11 is that banks with more risky assets are required to hold more capital to absorb any potential losses. Indeed, the correlation between RWA and different equity measures is very strong and positive in our sample, implying that most banks respond to a higher RWA by holding more capital.[34] However, these adjustments should make banks with different

---

[34] The correlation coefficients between RWA and different measures of equity (both

portfolio risks have comparable default risks.[35] In other words, the additional capital should be at least proportional to the increase of RWA, leading to a more horizontal (i.e. insignificant) relationship than in Figure 5.11. Moreover, Figure 5.12 shows that the relationship between Tier-1 capital ratio and portfolio risks is negative and not positive. In short, the willingness to hold more capital does not seem to explain why banks with presumably riskier portfolios (as measured by RWA) appear safer.

A more convincing answer to the question comes from a careful look into the business models depicted in Figure 5.11. All of the banks with high Z-scores and high RWA are retail banks. In turn, the banks on the other extreme of the relationship are more mixed, consisting mostly of investment and wholesale banks. It is therefore possible that some of these banks are engaging in regulatory arbitrage to ship risky assets off their balance sheets without actually transferring the risks, which is contributing to a low Z-score or proximity to default. The economics literature has only recently focused on analysing such practices in detail, identifying the use of structured products to achieve lower capital charges "without risk transfer"

---

as % of assets), including tier-1 capital, common equity, tangible common equity, and total equity, are approximately 0.70, implying a very strong positive relationship between the two sets of measures.

[35] Although empirical research supports the presence of a strong positive correlation between portfolio risk and capital, the impact of capital requirements on banks' default likelihood is far from clear (Shrieves & Dahl, 1992; Berger, 1995; Jacques & Nigro, 1997; Rime, 2001). The theoretical literature has suggested several explanations on why default probabilities may not be properly mitigated by capital requirements. Purely linear (i.e. un-weighted) capital requirements may increase bank failure likelihoods as risk-loving institutions reshuffle their portfolios in such a way to increase their overall risks (Kahane, 1977; Koehn & Santomero, 1980; Kim & Santomero, 1988). The use of improper or 'incorrect' risk-weights may also induce banks to engage in regulatory arbitrage and increase the likelihood of bank failure (Kim & Santomero, 1988; Rochet, 1992). Moreover, when limited liability is introduced, even the 'correct' risk-weighted capital requirements may not be sufficient to limit risk (Keeley & Furlong, 1990; Rochet, 1992). This is particularly the case for under-capitalised banks, where the shareholders may prefer to gamble the value of the bank by taking larger risks than they would in the absence of capital requirements. Lastly, more recent research has highlighted that higher capital may have the 'unintended effect' of allowing banks to take more tail risks while remaining compliant with regulatory requirements (Perotti et al., 2011).

(Acharya et al., 2010b).[36] If true, these arguments would also mean that RWAs are not a good measure of a bank's real risk exposures.

Figure 5.12 Relationship between Tier-1 ratio and RWA

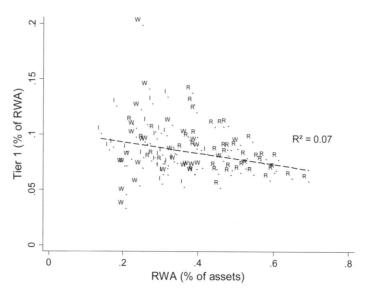

Notes: The letters R, I and W stand for the retail, investment and wholesale banking models. The coefficient estimate for RWA is significant at the 1% level.

Two findings give support to the idea that RWA may be an inaccurate measure that can be manipulated. First, in our sample there appears to be a weak (but statistically significant) negative relationship between earnings volatility and average risk weights. Indeed, Figure 5.13 shows that the standard deviation of the RoA is negatively correlated to mean RWA values. Therefore, it is likely that risk-weights are not accurately measuring the underlying volatility of a bank's earnings, which is a principle source of riskiness emanating from variability in returns from investments and loans. Second, Figure 5.14 confirms that some banks, especially those categorised under the investment banking model, may be using derivative transactions to reduce their RWA. The figure identifies the

---

[36] Jones (2000, p. 48) also raised the possibility that "recent innovations in credit derivatives and the design of [credit loan obligations], together with additional capital arbitrage opportunities ... are widely believed to afford large, sophisticated banks expanded opportunities for still further [regulatory capital arbitrage]".

existence of a relatively strong and positive correlation between the use of derivatives transactions and lowered RWA.[37] Provided that derivative transactions are an integral part of the construction and operation of structured products, the findings seem to give additional support to the idea that some of these activities may be used to reduce capital charges without adequately transferring risks.

Figure 5.13 Relationship between earnings volatility and RWA

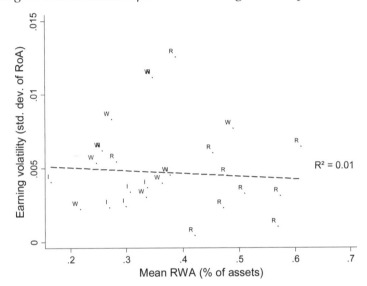

Notes: The letters R, I and W stand for the retail, investment and wholesale banking models. The coefficient estimate for mean RWA is only significant at the 10% level (p-value = 0.078). The diagram involves a reduced number of observations (sample size of 28) due to the use of standard deviation for the calculation of earnings volatility.

---

[37] It is important to note these findings cannot be used to concretely build up evidence against a specific bank or a banking model. They only indicate a reason to suspect that regulatory arbitrage may be used. As is usually the case in any avoidance or illegal activity, concrete evidence is extremely hard to come by and requires a deep analysis and investigation, which is beyond the aims of this study.

Figure 5.14 Relationship between derivative transactions and RWA

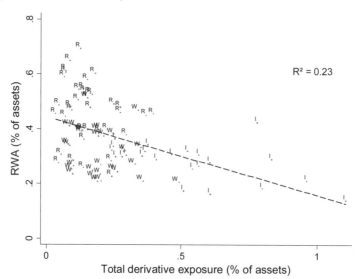

Notes: The letters R, I and W stand for the retail, investment and wholesale banking models. The coefficient estimate for total derivative exposures is significant at the 1% level.

To sum up, the results reviewed in this section show that the retail banking model has been the least risky. Although some of the indicators are open to interpretation, these banks appear to have the least inherent risks, as captured by the default likelihood estimates. In line with these observations, the retail banks have received less support than their peers during the crisis. Wholesale banks appear to be the most risky business model, followed by investment banks. Market-based risk measures appear to draw a less contrasting picture of riskiness, most likely reflecting the anticipation of a bail-out. Moreover, risk-weighted assets appear to be doing a poor job in identifying risks, supporting arguments of the UK's Independent Commission on Banking (2011, pp. 68-69). Some banks, including investment banks, may be taking advantage of this shortcoming by using derivative transactions to reduce their capital charges without achieving any risk transfer. However, a more convincing argument building on these issues requires a deeper and more detailed analysis, which is beyond the purpose of this study.

5.2.4 Corporate governance

The previous subsections have looked at the structure, performance and riskiness of the banking models identified in the study. This subsection turns to the distinct governance practices. The appropriateness and effectiveness of these practices are hard to identify due to a number of reasons, including the unavailability of comparable data. Nevertheless, an effort was made to investigate a diverse set of indicators to distinguish the business models.

Glancing through the indicators in Table 5.8, it is easy to see that some of the fundamental aspects of the three business models are confirmed by the findings. Retail banks spend more on audit fees, measured as a share of their assets. A substantial proportion of these fees (nearly one-third) are non-statutory fees, which predominantly take the form of fees from tax and legal advice. In turn, statutory audit fees represent nearly three-quarters of the total audit fees of investment banks and wholesale banks, implying their reliance on in-house legal and tax advice.

Table 5.8 Audit fees and executive compensation practices of business models

	Retail	Investment	Wholesale	All
Total audit fees (cents per '000 € of assets)	4.1 **	3.2 **	2.4 **	3.2
Statutory audit fees (cents per '000 € of assets)	2.8 **	2.5 **	1.8 **	2.3
Long-term bonus plan [a]	58.1% **	87.0% **	23.3% **	54.2%
Formal option plan	81.4% *	78.3% *	30.0% **	64.6%
Annual bonuses (% of annual pay) [b]	39.7% **	31.1% *	30.4% *	34.7%
Compensation committee	100.0% **	65.2% **	40.0% **	72.9%

Notes: All figures correspond to cluster and sample means.

[a] Long-term bonus plans are those that reward the CEOs with cash or shares, conditional on multiple-year performance criteria.

[b] Share of annual bonus (excluding long-term bonuses) in total annual pay. The independence of cluster subsamples was tested using the Wilcoxon-Mann-Whitney non-parametric two-sample tests at the 5% level of significance. According to these tests, a single asterisk (*) signifies statistical difference from a single cluster, i.e. the furthermost cluster; two asterisks (**) signify statistical difference from both clusters.

Figure 5.15 shows that total audit fees appear to have converged during the crisis. In particular, while retail banks have continually reduced the fees they pay (as a share of their assets). Meanwhile, the opposite holds for investment and wholesale banks. In particular, the total audit fees of wholesale banks increased by over 30% in 2009, mostly due to new non-statutory fees that may reflect the banks' troubles.

Figure 5.15 Evolution of total audit fees during crisis

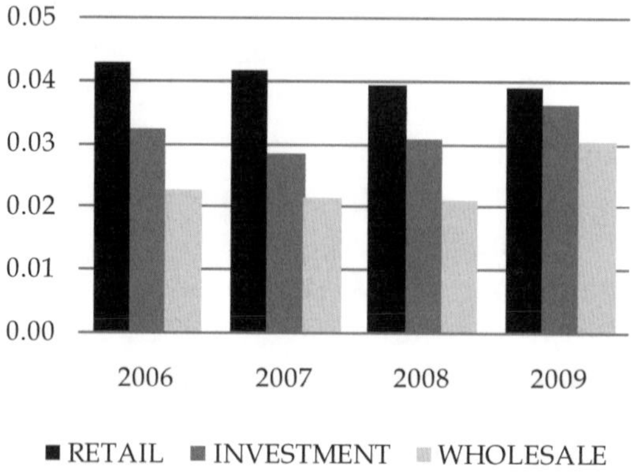

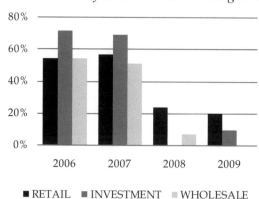

Note: All figures are expressed in € per €1,000 of assets.

For the sampled banks' executive compensation practices, Table 5.8 shows that wholesale banks are more likely to have traditional salary packages, consisting mostly of fixed pay. Interestingly, all retail banks and most investment banks have executive compensation boards. This finding could be explained by both types of banks' extensive use of long-term compensation plans. In particular, nearly all of the investment banks have some form of long-term bonus plans, which are all performance related. The use of options is also prevalent in the two business models. Over time, all banks have reduced the share of annual bonuses in total annual pay (Figure 5.16). This is largely in line with the developments in the aftermath of the crisis and the public scrutiny of executive compensation.

Figure 5.16 Evolution of annual bonuses during crisis

Note: Figures represent share of annual bonus (excluding long-term bonuses) in total annual pay.

Table 5.9 Ownership attributes of business models

	Retail	Investment	Wholesale	All
Shareholder value (SHV) bank	90.9% **	70.8% **	37.5% **	66.7%
Cooperative bank	9.1% **	0.0% **	27.5% **	13.9%
Savings bank	0.0% **	16.7% **	30.0% **	14.8%
State-owned bank [a]	0.0% **	29.2% *	25.0% *	15.7%
Private block owners (% owned) [b]	14.4% **	4.5% **	40.1% **	21.7%
Listed on stock exchange	90.9% **	79.2% **	47.5% **	72.2%

Notes: All figures are the mean values for the year-end observations for the relevant sample. The independence of cluster subsamples was tested using the Wilcoxon-Mann-Whitney non-parametric two-sample tests at 5% significance. According to these tests, a single asterisk (*) signifies statistical difference from a single cluster, i.e. the furthermost cluster; two asterisks (**) signify statistical difference from both clusters.

[a] At least 50% owned by public authorities.

[b] Private block owners are those that own more than a 5% stake, excluding the stakes of domestic public authorities.

Turning to banks' ownership structure, Table 5.9 shows that retail banks are more likely than their peers to be listed on the stock exchange, owned by their private shareholders. Indeed, more than 90% of all retail banks are listed. A substantial majority of the banks categorised as investment banks are also listed. Wholesale banks are the most mixed group, half comprising a more or less equivalent proportion of shareholder-value, cooperative and savings banks. More than half of these banks are unlisted on the stock exchanges.

Block ownership by private shareholders (i.e. shareholders with a minimum stake of 5%) also shows a substantial variation. On the one hand are wholesale banks in which the total stakes of block owners is nearly 40%, representing a substantial concentration of voting power and control. To a large extent, the predominance of block ownership in wholesale banks is due to the categorisation of a number of central network cooperative and savings institutions in this group. Unlike their commercial banks, these banks tend to be collectively owned by the local banks to which that they provide liquidity and other centralised services.[38]

---

[38] See Appendix III for individual bank cases involving central institutions. Also, see the discussion on the role of central institutions in cooperative banking networks in Ayadi et al. (2010, pp. 17-24).

Public authorities do not own any one of the retail banks in our sample. This is an interesting finding since the clustering analysis, which did not consider any one of the ownership attributes, managed to clearly distinguish a group of banks that are entirely privately-owned. In turn, approximately one-quarter of all wholesale and investment banks are state-owned. As Figure 5.17 clearly depicts, some of the publicly-owned investment and wholesale banks are those that are nationalised or partly-nationalised due to their troubles during the crisis. Nevertheless, the figure shows that state-ownership was common in these two models even before the crisis.

Figure 5.17 Evolution of state ownership during crisis

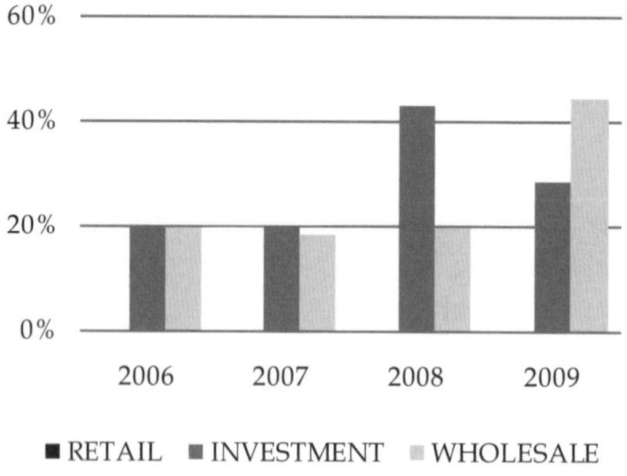

Notes: All figures are the mean values for the year-end observations for the relevant sample. State ownership is defined as a minimum 50% ownership. None of the retail banks were state-owned in the sample period.

To sum up, an assessment of governance practices does not reveal any particular strengths or weaknesses of the business models. Retail banks appear to use more legal and tax advice externally although the differences between the business models have diminished during the crisis. In terms of executive compensation, wholesale banks use more fixed pay while both retail and investment banks provide long-term packages. The use of annual bonuses has declined substantially during the crisis; however, more information on other packages is needed to assess fully whether this is equivalent to a more predominant use of fixed pay. In terms of their ownership structures, retail banks are more likely to be listed on the stock exchange. Wholesale banks are more likely to be 'central network institutions',[39] which are owned by their local savings or cooperative institutions. Lastly, public ownership, which does not apply to any of the retail banks, has increased in recent years for wholesale and investment banks due to nationalisations.

5.2.5 Disclosure practices

The last area for the evaluation of the different business models is disclosure practices. The data for constructing the relevant measures come from the database that forms the basis of this study. A number of variables were chosen from a set of categories that span across the banks' financial performance, financial position, risk exposure, accounting policies and governance practices. The indicators are typically used by the IMF and the World Bank to evaluate banks' soundness.[40]

Table 5.10 provides an overview of the indicators used to construct the transparency indices. Most of the indicators have been used throughout this report. Others have not been presented, in many cases due to low coverage ratios. More in detail, the variables relating to financial performance assess the profitability, cost-efficiency and income sources of the banks. The variables related to financial position provide an understanding of the main strategies and conditions of the bank, focusing mainly on capital conditions. Risk exposure variables provide an understanding of where the main risks lie. Accounting and governance policies are more descriptive and provide a general understanding of the relevant topics.

It is important to note that some of the indicators discussed in the study have not been included in the list of variables. In particular, the variables were chosen based on their availability. For example, variables such as total assets, type of ownership, total net income, total customer deposits, etc. are standard and are not considered part of the transparency measure. Other variables that could prove useful, such as term structure of deposits (sight, time, etc.), debt maturity, etc., were not included since most banks did not report such data.[41] In short, the indicators were built just to

---

[39] See Ayadi et al. (2010) for more on this concept.

[40] See World Bank/IMF (2005) for an overview.

[41] As a general rule, no variable with less than 10% coverage was included in the transparency indicator.

allow a comparison of the different models in this study and not to serve as a stand-alone measure of transparency.

Table 5.10 Variables used for assessing data disclosure

Category	Variable	Category	Variable
Financial performance	Return on assets (RoA)	Risk exposure	Loans to banks
	Return on equity (RoE)		Loans to customers
	Cost-to-income ratio (CIR)		Loans to public authorities
	Interest margin		Domestic assets
	Non-interest income		Derivatives, positive fair value
	Income tax		Derivatives, negative fair value
Financial position	Risk-weighted assets		Cash and balances with central bank
	Total regulatory capital		
	Tier 1 capital		Reverse repurchase agreements
	Tier 2 capital		Repurchase agreements
	Tier 3 capital	Accounting policies	Accounting firm
	Subordinated debt		Accounting method
	Goodwill		Total audit fee
	Common equity		Statutory audit fee
	Tangible common equity	Governance practices	Annual bonuses
	Common leverage ratio		Compensation committee
	Issuance of new shares		Corporate social responsibility report

Table 5.11 provides a comparison of the three models in terms of their data disclosure practices. All banks are relatively open about their financial performances. Most banks, especially the listed entities, are forthcoming to make their performance public. Investment banks are more transparent in the aggregate, in particular in disclosing data on their financial positions and risk exposures. In turn, wholesale banks are less transparent, especially in their governance practices. Retail banks are in between these two models, providing the most information on their governance practices.

Glancing generally over the figures, the most striking result is possibly the lack of detailed information on risk exposures. Despite the intention to choose non-trivial variables, the annual reports and financial statements of most banks contain very little detailed information on the risk exposures of banks. What is more, it is very hard to distinguish the banks based on their business models. Indeed, with the exception of financial position, all categories include some statistical ties, i.e. cases where the performances of two business models are not significantly different.

Table 5.11 Data disclosure practices of business models

	Retail	Investment	Wholesale	All
Financial performance	99.1%*	96.6%**	99.2%*	98.6%
Financial position	79.7%**	84.9%**	74.1%**	78.8%
Risk exposure	50.4%*	56.1%**	52.9%*	52.6%
Accounting policies	89.4%*	84.7%*	97.5%**	91.4%
Governance	88.3%*	85.4%*	64.6%**	78.9%
ALL CATEGORIES	72.0%**	74.2%**	68.8%**	71.3%

Notes: All figures correspond to cluster and sample means. The independence of cluster subsamples was tested using the Wilcoxon-Mann-Whitney non-parametric two-sample tests at the 5% level of significance. According to these tests, a single asterisk (*) signifies statistical difference from a single cluster, i.e. the furthermost cluster; two asterisks (**) signify statistical difference from both clusters.

Although recent amendments to the Capital Requirements Directive (CRD) have addressed disclosure requirements on securitisation and remuneration policies, our data collection reveals that public information on even the simplest variables is incomplete. This is particularly the case for risk exposures, which is contributing to the low score of our sample. For example, only 28% of the sampled banks report the share of total loans to public bodies. Moreover, only half of the banks make any distinction between domestic and international loans. It is important to note that lack of adequate disclosure on risk exposure is not limited to the variables included in Table 5.10 or covered by the database for the study. For example, although an EU-wide standard on the definition of SMEs is available (Recommendation 2003/361/EC), loans to SMEs are not a standard part of public disclosures of banks. Most banks do not report any information on their currency exposures, not to mention their international exposures. In addition, maturities are likewise rarely available of underlying assets and liabilities, which are set to become an important part of the regulatory framework proposed by the Basel Committee on Banking Supervision (BCBS) under the Basel III.[42]

---

[42] Citing similar difficulties with data availability, IMF (2011, p. 78) notes that it could not evaluate the liquidity coverage ratio proposed by the BCBS under Basel III "because it required information on the credit quality, ratings, and liquidity characteristics of the ratio's so-called Level II assets—such as covered bonds, rated corporate bonds, and agency debt—that are not publicly available".

As another sticking point, there appears to be little congruity in the information that is made public. Even simple items, such as loans to and deposits from customers, may cover different counterparties, excluding or including other financial institutions. Similarly, many banks did not provide consistent data on their full-time equivalent headcounts. As another example, cash and cash-like assets were treated differently, in some cases not properly distinguishing them from reserves at the national central banks. There was also no homogeneity on the definition of non-performing loans, i.e. arrears, doubtful loans, repossessions, etc., which undermines the comparability of any available information.

To sum up, the results suggest that transparency could be improved substantially if banks were required to disclose more (standardised) information on their risk exposure and financial position. Although it is hard to single out any specific model, wholesale banks can also be required to reveal more information on their governance practices, in particular details on their executive compensation.

6. CONCLUSIONS

To summarise the main results, the banks that are identified as falling within the 'retail banking model' are those institutions that are the least leveraged and have taken fewer risks, while performing comparably and with better governance practices than their peers. Most of these institutions are commercially-owned, i.e. 'shareholder-value' (SHV) institutions, providing traditional services, such as retail deposits and loans, to the general public. Although most of the banks that received state aid have agreed to reorient their activities towards a more retail banking model, our results do not show that this has taken place. In fact, many retail banks have moved closer to wholesale and investment banking models in recent years.

Investment banks are also the mostly commercially-oriented. These banks are among the most leveraged (i.e. low proportion of tangible common equity to total assets) and engage extensively in trading activities while relying on short-term funding and lending, such as repos and reverse repos transactions. Most provide long-term bonus plans or option plans to their executives. The investment banks' performance has fluctuated substantially during the crisis. As a consequence, many have received extensive state support or have become nationalised. However, their trading losses have been moderate and earnings appear to have bounced back in 2009.

Wholesale banks have a more mixed ownership structure, comprising many cooperative or savings central network institutions. Owing to the nature of their activities, most of these banks specialise in wholesale banking, providing services to public sector entities, other financial institutions and large and middle-sized corporations. The wholesale banks have performed remarkably worse than their peers according to many measures, many receiving some form of state support or becoming nationalised in the years 2008 and 2009. Interestingly, trading losses (and cost-inefficiencies) were the main explanatory factors for these results. Apart from showing the severity of the conditions faced by wholesale banks, the results also called into question the economic wisdom of diversifying into these non-core areas of activity.

An interesting finding that emerges from the study is that market-based indicators of risk, such as CDS spreads, cannot be used to distinguish between the underlying risks faced by the three banking models. It appears that the moral hazard issues that arise from the potential for state support for too-big-to-fail institutions may bias market-based measures, rendering them less useful for regulatory purposes or for identifying underlying risks for each bank. Moreover, there is no coherent relationship between the estimates of likely default derived from banks' financial statements and the risk-weights applied in compliance with regulatory requirements. In short, the results raise concerns over the use of different measures of risk. A more detailed study of bank riskiness was not possible due to the limited amount of data available.

Several observations can be made concerning the impact of upcoming regulations in light of the findings of this study.

First, the results provide some justification to the recent popularised view that the retail banking model is safer than the others. Despite their commercial orientation and their size, these banks were safer than their peers and have performed relatively well before, during and after the crisis. Our findings also point to some weaknesses of the institutions in the investment banking model, which tend to rely on less stable funding sources, engage heavily in trading activities and maintain a very low share of loss-absorbing capital compared to the other two models (i.e. common tangible capital) despite comparable Tier-1 ratios. In turn, the wholesale banking group appears to be the most risky, possibly arising from a lower share of liquid assets and a greater use of more volatile interbank funding. In this sense, the capital requirements that focus on more loss-absorbing capital, especially in the definition of leverage ratios, and on the use of more traditional forms of funding and liquidity management (such as the net stable funding ratio – NFSR) could be useful in reducing the inherent risks in banking.

Second, the fact that most of the banks in our sample, including nearly half of the retail banks, have received government support in one form or another is likely to invite moral hazard problems. Indeed, although various measures point to differing underlying risks, the market's pricing of default probabilities (via CDS spreads) are virtually identical on average for the three business models. This implies that the market participants see no reason to distinguish between the inherent risks of different business models, possibly in anticipation of the eventual government support that the sampled banks would receive. These findings call for a serious investigation into the use of additional capital charges for "systemically important financial institutions" or SIFIs. Implementing a Financial Stability Contribution (FSC), as proposed by the IMF (2010) and partly supported by the European Commission (COM(2010) 254), to internalise the cost of crises and facilitate crisis management in the EU may also address the risks arising from 'too-big-to-fail' institutions.

Third, a heavy reliance on risk-adjusted capital requirements may be misguided since the risk-weights appear to be unrelated, and even inversely linked, to underlying risks. Although the results of the study have to be interpreted with care, there is concern that certain banks may use their specialisation in trading activities to offload some of the riskier portions of their assets from their balance sheets without actually reducing their inherent risks. This gives additional justification for the use of simple rules, such as the proposed leverage ratio as called for under the Basel III framework.[43]

Fourth, it is necessary for banks to disclose more information publicly and in a coherent manner. In particular, there is little information on details regarding their activities, in particular their risk exposures to different sectors, customer classes and off-balance sheet entities. For investors and deposit-holders to engage in proper monitoring of the banks, more relevant disclosure is needed on these items. Although some banks provide extensive information on these items, the data are far from comparable. Standardisation and reinforcement of disclosure requirements for a core set of items in line with international accounting standards could be very useful in allowing investors to obtain a proper understanding of the risks and to make comparisons between different financial institutions. In this sense, it may be advisable to give new impetus to the required use of electronic standards, such as the XBRL (eXtensible Business Reporting Language) in supervisory reporting. Another policy that can enhance the availability of reliable information on banks is the public dissemination of supervisory data, as is the case for many banks in the US.

---

[43] An alternative would be to oblige banks to hold much more capital than is currently required. Indeed, a recent study has found that the socially 'optimal' capital requirement would be around 20% of the RWA (Miles et al., 2011).

Lastly, the one-time monitoring exercise undertaken by this study is bound to be incomplete, especially in view of the missing post-crisis data. Among other elements that need to be monitored, one important issue that deserves attention is the extent to which the banks that received state aid re-orient themselves towards other models. Moreover, it could be useful to enlarge the scope of the study to a larger set of banks and to extend the research back further to the early 2000s, all in an attempt to acquire a deeper understanding of the pre- and post-crisis evolution of the banking models. For these purposes, the current study may well serve as a first step towards a more regular monitoring of the EU's banking sector.

The following table summarises the main policy recommendations presented above.

Table 6.1 Main recommendations of the study

Observations	Recommended policy responses
Highly leveraged institutions and wide discrepancies in loss-absorbing capital	Introduce leverage ratio and focus more on loss-absorbing capital definition as proposed under Basel III framework
Excessive reliance on short-term funding in investment and wholesale-oriented banks	Introduce incentives for stable funding, i.e. NFSR and liquidity ratio under Basel III framework
Market does not distinguish between business models despite notable differences in risks	Require more capital from SIFIs and/or implement FSC charges to banks to address 'too-big-to-fail' risks
Risk-weighted assets may not be linked to underlying risks and may be manipulated	Supplement current approach with un-weighted capital requirements, i.e. leverage ratio under Basel III framework
Incomplete and incoherent disclosure in public statements, especially on risk exposure	Consider giving impetus to the implementation of standard disclosure formats, i.e. XBRL, and public dissemination of supervisory data as in the US
Missing post-crisis data and changing business models	Initiate regular monitoring exercise

7. CHANGING BUSINESS MODELS OF BANKS IN THE POST-CRISIS ERA

The evolution of European banking and its business models over the coming years is likely to be dominated by the legacy of the crisis and the regulatory and supervisory responses to it. Our analysis suggests that the aftermath of the crisis will be transformational in four major dimensions: 1) the size and growth of the banking industry, 2) in bank business models, 3) with respect to financial system structure and above all, 4) in all aspects of the regulatory regime.

Regarding the relative size of the banking industry, it is likely that the banking industry is entering a period of slower growth than in the years prior to the onset of the crisis. This is largely because the 'excess financialisation' and the factors giving rise to it, noted in section 2, are likely to be reversed, not the least because it proved to be unsustainable. Two reasons for this will be the unwinding of some of the factors that previously induced the unsustainable growth trends of the past – most especially the requirement for banks to hold more equity capital – and the likelihood that the cost of capital will also rise as, in some respects, the cost of capital was artificially low in the period before the crisis. Banks are also likely to give more rigorous attention to the risk characteristics of their business. As banks adjust to a regime of higher capitalisation, the de-leveraging process will impact on the growth of bank lending. These factors will influence the growth of banking on the supply side of the equation. If, as argued below, banking will become more expensive for a wide range of customers, slower growth may also emanate from the demand side. In many ways, some aspects of banking (including risk) were significantly under-priced and this is likely to be reversed. Overall, therefore, banks across Europe will give more attention to the risk characteristics of their business models and in the pricing of risk.

As a result of these changes, there will inevitably be some 'displacement' of business that was previously channelled through the balance sheet of banks. This is likely to include more business gravitating to the capital market which, in its turn, will change some aspects of bank business models, as some banks will be in a position to facilitate their corporate customers making debt issues in the markets and assisting customers' capital market operations in various other ways. While the securitisation market is largely closed at present, this is likely to be a temporary phenomenon and banks will again seek to securitise some of their lending – albeit (and partly under regulatory pressure) in different ways than in the past, most especially with respect to their having to retain at least some of the credit risk. Another phenomenon that may grow in the future is the institutional cash pools from the demand-side perspective.[44] Today, although these new forms of shadow banking seem to prioritise safety and diversification over yield, this may not be the case in the future.

With regard specifically to business models, it is likely that there will be some reversion to more traditional banking models with, for instance, a greater emphasis on the more stable retail funding of banks' balance sheet positions in combination with lesser reliance than in the pre-crisis period on wholesale funding activities. The regulatory demand for banks to become more liquid will itself encourage a greater focus on retail funding as well as a requirement to hold more liquid assets on the balance sheet. It is generally regarded that too little attention (including by regulators) has been given to the liquidity aspects of banks' business operations.

It is also likely that banks will come under pressure (not least from regulators) to operate with less complex business structures. This can be seen, for instance, in the requirement to create living wills so that key parts of a banking business can be ring-fenced and more easily resolvable in the event of a bank becoming distressed. This is part of a strategy in the evolving regulatory regime to be able to manage the resolution of distressed banks in a more orderly, coherent, timely and predictable manner.

If, as argued, banking will become less expansionary compared with the pre-crisis period, it is also likely that banking will become more expensive, partly because of the higher regulatory costs (capital, etc.), but

---

[44] See Pozsar (2011).

also because more realistic and sustainable risk pricing is likely to emerge. It is also feasible that some banks will become more risk averse.

Overall, it is unlikely that banking will be as profitable in the coming years as it appeared to be in the pre-crisis period although, to a large extent, this was largely illusory because risk was being under-priced and many of the banking strategies that emerged in the previous period proved to be unsustainable. This is not to say that the current relatively low profitability will not be reversed, but rather that profitability is not likely to regain its pre-crisis levels. All this in turn suggests that banks will be under ever more pressure to manage their costs and this, in the course of time, is likely to induce more consolidation in the European banking industry so as to gain alleged economies of scale.

As hinted at in an earlier chapter, a major driving force in the future evolution and business models and strategies of banks will be regulation and supervision. In some senses this could be the dominant driver in the coming years as banks are forced to adjust to a more demanding regulatory and supervisory environment. Predictably, banks are already raising concerns about the potential costs of regulation and not the least those that allegedly derive from higher capital (most especially equity) requirements. Just as the crisis has been the most severe and far-reaching than for many decades (with some arguing, for instance the chairman of the UK's Financial Services Authority, that it has been the most serious banking crisis "in the history of capitalism"), so it is likely that it will induce one of the most substantial sets of changes ever in the regulatory and supervisory regime. The changes will be far-reaching and will include, inter alia:

- The requirement to hold more capital, especially equity capital,
- Enhanced loss-absorbing capability including bail-ins, contingent capital, etc.
- A minimum leverage ratio on top of the risk-weighted capital requirements,
- Differential (higher) capital requirements imposed on banks that are deemed to be systemically significant with the implication that large banks will need to hold more capital than other institutions and
- More onerous liquidity requirements.

Overall, these requirements are likely to induce slower growth in banking, higher costs and lower profitability.

As well as formal regulatory requirements, banks will also be subject to more intensive and extensive supervision. There will be increased supervisory attention to banks' business models and a greater focus on testing banks' risk models and their risk analysis and management systems. Supervisors are likely to become more interventionist in their approach, which will include judgements about business models, the way that business models are managed and operated, and banks' internal incentive structures especially with regard to bonus payments and how they are calculated. Several supervisory agencies have already announced that they will monitor the extent to which internal reward structures create incentives for excessive risk-taking. There will also likely be more attention given to governance arrangements within banks including monitoring the expertise of senior bankers. The latter was cited by the incoming head of the UK's prudential agency at a public meeting in London on 19 May 2011.

Business models will also likely change as the centre of gravity in the world economy shifts most especially regarding the continued growth of emerging market economies, which will create new business opportunities and strategies for some banks.

All these pressures will impact differently on different banks according to their business profiles. Whilst it is impossible to predict precisely how business models will change for different types of banks, there is little doubt that the implications will be substantial. Our judgement, however, is that European banking will not converge on a single business model. Diversity will remain with the spectrum of models including fully-diversified banks, comprehensive financial conglomerates, retail financial conglomerates, core-cluster institutions, specialist banks, niche-segmentation institutions, joint ventures, etc.

REFERENCES

Acharya, V.V., D. Gale and T. Yorulmazer (2010), "Rollover Risk and Market Freezes", NBER Working Papers, No. 15674, National Bureau of Economic Research, Cambridge, MA.

Acharya, V.V., P. Schnabl and G. Suarez (2010), "Securitization without risk transfer", NBER Working Papers, No. 15730, National Bureau of Economic Research, Cambridge, MA.

Acharya, V.V. and S. Viswanathan (2011), "Leverage, Moral Hazard, and Liquidity", *Journal of Finance*, Vol. 66, No. 1, pp. 99-138.

Adrian, T. and H.S. Shin (2008), "Financial Intermediary Leverage and Value-at-Risk", Federal Reserve Bank of New York Staff Reports, No. 338, Federal Reserve Bank of New York, New York, NY.

_____ (2010), "Liquidity and Leverage", *Journal of Financial Intermediation*, Vol. 19, No. 3, pp. 418-437.

Allessandri, P. and A. Haldane (2009), "Banking on the State", Bank of England, London.

Ayadi, R., E. Arbak and W.P. de Groen (forthcoming), "Executive Compensation and Risk-Taking in European Banking", in J.R. Barth, C. Lin and C. Wihlborg (eds), *Research Handbook for Banking and Governance*, Cheltenham: Edward Elgar Publishing.

Ayadi, R. and P. Behr (2009), "On the Necessity to Regulate Credit Derivatives Markets", *Journal of Banking Regulation*, Vol. 10, No. 3, pp. 179-201.

Ayadi, R., D.T. Llewelyn, R.H. Schmidt, E. Arbak and W.P. de Groen (2010), *Investigating Diversity in the Banking Sector in Europe: Key Developments, Performance and Role of Cooperative Banks*, Centre for European Policy Studies (CEPS), Brussels.

Ayadi, R., R.H. Schmidt, S. Carbo Valverde, E. Arbak and F. Rodriguez Fernandez (2009), *Investigating Diversity in the Banking Sector in Europe: The Performance and Role of Savings Banks*, Centre for European Policy Studies (CEPS), Brussels.

Baele, L., O. De Jonghe and R. Vander Vennet (2007), "Does the Stock Market Value Bank Diversification?", *Journal of Banking and Finance*, Vol. 31, No. 7, pp. 1999-2023.

Barth, J.R., R.D. Brumbaugh Jr. and J.A. Wilcox (2000), "The Repeal of Glass-Steagall and the Advent of Broad Banking", OCC Economic Working

Paper, No. 2000-5, US Office of the Comptroller of the Currency, Washington, D.C., April.

Benston, G.J., W.C. Hunter and L.D. Wall (1995), "Motivations for Bank Mergers and Acquisitions: Enhancing the Deposit Insurance Put Option versus Earnings Diversification", *Journal of Money, Credit, and Banking*, Vol. 27, No. 3, pp. 777-788.

Bernanke, B., M. Gertler and S. Gilchrist (1996), "The Financial Accelerator and the Flight to Quality", *Review of Economics and Statistics*, Vol. 78, No. 1, pp. 1-15.

Berger, A.N. (1995), "The Relationship between Capital and Earnings in Banking", *Journal of Money, Credit, and Banking*, Vol. 27, No. 2, pp. 432-456.

Boyd, J.H. and D.E. Runkle (1993), "Size and Performance of Banking Firms: Testing the Predictions of Theory", *Journal of Monetary Economics*, Vol. 31, No. 1, pp. 47-67.

Boot, A.W. and A.V. Thakor (2009), "The Accelerating Integration of Banks and Markets and its Implications for Regulation", in A. Berger, P. Molyneux and J. Wilson (eds), *The Oxford Handbook of Banking*, Oxford: Oxford University Press.

Brunnermeier, M.K. (2009), "Symposium: Early Stages of the Credit Crunch: Deciphering the Liquidity and Credit Crunch 2007-2008", *Journal of Economic Perspectives*, Winter, Vol. 23, No. 1, pp. 77-100.

Calinski, R.B. and J. Harabasz (1974), "A dendrite method for cluster analysis", *Communications in Statistics*, Vol. 3, No. 1, pp. 1-27.

Calomiris, C.W. (1999), "Building an Incentive-Compatible Safety Net", *Journal of Banking and Finance*, Vol. 23, No. 10, pp. 1499-1519.

Calomiris, C.W. and C.M. Kahn (1991), "The Role of Demandable Debt in Structuring Optimal Banking Arrangements", *American Economic Review*, Vol. 81, No. 3, pp. 497-513.

Čihák, M. and H. Hesse (2007), "Cooperative Banks and Financial Stability", IMF Working Papers, No. WP/07/02, International Monetary Fund, Washington, D.C.

Dell'Ariccia, G., E. Friedman and R. Marquez (1999), "Adverse Selection as a Barrier to Entry in the Banking Industry", *RAND Journal of Economics*, Autumn, Vol. 30, No. 3, pp. 515-534.

Demirgüç-Kunt, A. and H. Huizinga (2010a), "Are banks too big to fail or too big to save? International evidence from equity prices and CDS spreads", World Bank Policy Research Working Paper Series, No. 5360, World Bank, Washington, D.C.

_____ (2010b), "Bank Activity and Funding Strategies: The Impact on Risk and Returns", *Journal of Financial Economics*, Vol. 98, No. 3, pp. 626-650.

Demsetz, R.S. and P.E. Strahan (1997), "Diversification, Size, and Risk at Bank Holding Companies", *Journal of Money, Credit and Banking*, Vol. 29, No. 3, pp. 300-313.

Desrochers, M. and K.P. Fischer (2005), "The Power of Networks: Integration and Financial Cooperative Performance", *Annals of Public and Cooperative Economics*, Vol. 76, No. 3, pp. 307-354.

DeYoung, R. and K.P. Roland (2001), "Product Mix and Earnings Volatility at Commercial Banks: Evidence from a Degree of Total Leverage Model", *Journal of Financial Intermediation*, Vol. 10, No. 1, pp. 54-84.

Diamond, D.W. (1984), "Financial Intermediation and Delegated Monitoring", *Review of Economic Studies*, Vol. 51, No. 3, pp. 393-414.

_____ (1991), "Monitoring and Reputation: The Choice between Bank Loans and Directly Placed Debt", *Journal of Political Economy*, Vol. 99, No. 4, pp. 689-721.

Diamond, D.W. and R.G. Rajan (2001), "Liquidity Risk, Liquidity Creation, and Financial Fragility: A Theory of Banking", *Journal of Political Economy*, Vol. 109, No. 2, pp. 287-327.

Duffee, G.R. and C. Zhou (2001), "Credit Derivatives in Banking: Useful Tools for Managing Risk?", *Journal of Monetary Economics*, Vol. 48, No. 1, pp. 25-54.

ECB (2010), *EU Banking Structures*, European Central Bank, Frankfurt.

Everitt, B.S., S. Landau and M. Leese (2001), *Cluster Analysis*, Fourth Edition, West Sussex: Wiley, John & Sons Ltd.

Flannery, M.J. and S.M. Sorescu (1996), "Evidence of Bank Market Discipline in Subordinated Debenture Yields: 1983-1991", *Journal of Finance*, Vol. 51, No. 4, pp. 1347-1377.

Focarelli, D., D. Marques-Ibanez and A.F. Pozzolo (2011), "Are universal banks better underwriters? Evidence from the last days of the Glass-Steagall Act", ECB Working Paper Series, No. 1287, European Central Bank, Frankfurt.

Gorton, G.B. and A. Metrick (forthcoming), "Securitized banking and the run on repo", *Journal of Financial Economics*.

Gorton, G.B. and G.G. Pennacchi (1995), "Banks and Loan Sales: Marketing Nonmarketable Assets", *Journal of Monetary Economics*, Vol. 35, No. 3, pp. 389-411.

Gorton, G.B., N.S. Souleles, M. Carey and R.M. Stulz (2006), "Special Purpose Vehicles and Securitization", in *The Risks of Financial Institutions*, A

National Bureau of Economic Research Conference Report, Chicago and London: University of Chicago Press, pp. 549-597.

Greenlaw, D., J. Hatzius, A.K. Kashyap and H.S. Shin (2008), "Leveraged Losses: Lessons from the Mortgage Market Meltdown", US Monetary Policy Forum Report, No. 2, Rosenberg Institute, Brandeis International Business School and Initiative on Global Markets, University of Chicago Graduate School of Business.

Haldane, A. (2009), "Rethinking the Financial Network", speech to Financial Student Association, Amsterdam, April (http://www.bankofengland.co.uk/publications/speeches/2009/speech409.pdf).

Huang, R. and L. Ratnovski (2010), "The Dark Side of Bank Wholesale Funding", IMF Working Papers, No. 10/170, International Monetary Fund, Washington, D.C.

IMF (2010), "A Fair and Substantial Contribution by the Financial Sector: Interim Report for the G-20", International Monetary Fund, Washington, D.C., April.

_____ (2011), "Global Financial Stability Report: Durable Financial Stability: Getting There from Here", International Monetary Fund, Washington, D.C.

Independent Commission on Banking (2011), "Interim Report: Consultation on Reform Options", London, April.

Jacques, K. and P. Nigro (1997), "Risk-Based Capital, Portfolio Risk, and Bank Capital: A Simultaneous Equations Approach", *Journal of Economics and Business*, Vol. 49, No. 6, pp. 533-547.

Jensen, M.C. (1986), "Agency Costs of Free Cash Flow, Corporate Finance, and Takeovers", *American Economic Review*, Vol. 76, No. 2, pp. 323-329.

Jensen, M.C. and W.H. Meckling (1976), "Theory of the Firm: Managerial Behavior, Agency Costs and Ownership Structure", *Journal of Financial Economics*, Vol. 3, No. 4, pp. 305-360.

Jones, D. (2000), "Emerging Problems with the Basel Capital Accord: Regulatory Capital Arbitrage and Related Issues", *Journal of Banking and Finance*, Vol. 24, Nos. 1-2, pp. 35-58.

Kahane, Y. (1977), "Capital adequacy and the regulation of financial intermediaries", *Journal of Banking and Finance*, Vol. 1, No. 2, pp. 207-218.

Kanatas, G. and J. Qi (1998), "Underwriting by Commercial Banks: Incentive Conflicts, Scope Economies, and Project Quality", *Journal of Money, Credit, and Banking*, Vol. 30, No. 1, pp. 119-133.

Kane, E.J. (2000), "Incentives for Banking Megamergers: What Motives Might Regulators Infer from Event-Study Evidence?", *Journal of Money, Credit, and Banking*, Vol. 32, No. 3, pp. 671-701.

Keeley, M.C. and F.T. Furlong (1990), "A Re-examination of Mean-Variance Analysis of Bank Capital Regulation", *Journal of Banking and Finance*, Vol. 14, No. 1, pp. 69-84.

Keys, B.J., T. Mukherjee, A. Seru and V. Vig (2010), "Did Securitization Lead to Lax Screening? Evidence from Subprime Loans", *Quarterly Journal of Economics*, Vol. 125, No. 1, pp. 307-362.

Kim, D. and A.M. Santomero (1988), "Risk in Banking and Capital Regulation", *Journal of Finance*, Vol. 43, No. 5, pp. 1219-1233.

Koehn, M. and A.M. Santomero (1980), "Regulation of Bank Capital and Portfolio Risk", *Journal of Finance*, Vol. 35, No. 5, pp. 1235-1244.

Kroszner, R.S. and R.G. Rajan (1994), "Is the Glass-Steagall Act Justified? A Study of the U.S. Experience with Universal Banking before 1933", *American Economic Review*, Vol. 84, No. 4, pp. 810-832.

Lang, W.W. and L.I. Nakamura (1995), "'Flight to Quality' in Banking and Economic Activity", *Journal of Monetary Economics*, Vol. 36, No. 1, pp. 145-164.

Llewellyn, D.T. (1999), *The New Economics of Banking*, SUERF Study, No. 5, SUERF, Vienna.

_____ (2010), "The Global Banking Crisis and the Post-Crisis Banking and Regulatory Scenario", Research Papers in Corporate Finance, University of Amsterdam.

Marquez, R. (2002), "Competition, Adverse Selection, and Information Dispersion in the Banking Industry", *Review of Financial Studies*, Summer, Vol. 15, No. 3, pp. 901-926.

Mian, A. and A. Sufi (2009), "The Consequences of Mortgage Credit Expansion: Evidence from the U.S. Mortgage Default Crisis", *Quarterly Journal of Economics*, Vol. 124, No. 4, pp. 1449-1496.

Miles, D., J. Yang and G. Marcheggiano (2011), "Optimal bank capital", Discussion Paper, No. 31, Bank of England, External Monetary Policy Committee (MPC) Unit, London.

Milligan, G.W. (1981), "A Review of Monte Carlo Tests of Cluster Analysis", *Multivariate Behavioral Research*, Vol. 16, No. 3.

Milligan, G.W. and M.C. Cooper (1985), "An Examination of Procedures for Determining the Number of Clusters in a Data Set", *Psychometrika*, Vol. 50, No. 2, pp. 159-179.

Myers, S.C. (1977), "Determinants of Corporate Borrowing", *Journal of Financial Economics*, Vol. 5, No. 2, pp. 147-175.

Myers, S.C. and N.S. Majluf (1984), "Corporate Financing and Investment Decisions When Firms Have Information That Investors Do Not Have", *Journal of Financial Economics*, Vol. 13, No. 2, pp. 187-221.

Neal, R.S. (1996), "Credit Derivatives: New Financial Instruments for Controlling Credit Risk", *Federal Reserve Bank of Kansas City Economic Review*, 2nd Quarter, Vol. 81, No. 2, pp. 14-27.

O'Hara, M. and W. Shaw (1990), "Deposit Insurance and Wealth Effects: The Value of Being 'Too Big to Fail'", *Journal of Finance*, Vol. 45, No. 5, pp. 1587-1600.

Penas, M.F. and H. Unal (2004), "Gains in Bank Mergers: Evidence from the Bond Markets", *Journal of Financial Economics*, Vol. 74, No. 1, pp. 149-179.

Perotti, E., L. Ratnovski and R. Vlahu (2011), "Capital Regulation and Tail Risk", Tinbergen Institute Discussion Papers: 11-039/DSF 14, Tinbergen Institute.

Pozsar, Z. (2011), "Institutional cash pools and the Triffin dilemma of the US banking system", IMF Working Paper 11/190, International Monetary Fund, Washington, D.C.

Pozsar, Z., T. Adrian, A. Ashcraft and H. Boesky (2010), "Shadow Banking", Staff Reports, No. 458, Federal Reserve Bank of New York Staff Reports, New York, NY, July.

Puri, M. (1994), "The Long-Term Default Performance of Bank Underwritten Security Issues", *Journal of Banking and Finance*, Vol. 18, No. 2, pp. 397-418.

Rajan, R.G. (1992), "Insiders and Outsiders: The Choice between Informed and Arm's-Length Debt", *Journal of Finance*, Vol. 47, No. 4, pp. 1367-1400.

Rime, B. (2001), "Capital Requirements and Bank Behaviour: Empirical Evidence for Switzerland", *Journal of Banking and Finance*, Vol. 25, No. 4, pp. 789-805.

Rochet, J.-C. (1992), "Capital Requirements and the Behaviour of Commercial Banks", *European Economic Review*, Vol. 36, No. 5, pp. 1137-1170.

Rochet, J.-C. and J. Tirole (1996), "Interbank Lending and Systemic Risk", *Journal of Money, Credit, and Banking*, Vol. 28, No. 4, pp. 733-762.

Sharpe, S.A. (1990), "Asymmetric Information, Bank Lending, and Implicit Contracts: A Stylized Model of Customer Relationships", *Journal of Finance*, Vol. 45, No. 4, pp. 1069-1087.

Shin, H.S. (2009), "Securitisation and Financial Stability", *Economic Journal*, Vol. 119, No. 536, pp. 309-332.

Shrieves, R.E. and D. Dahl (1992), "The Relationship between Risk and Capital in Commercial Banks", *Journal of Banking and Finance*, Vol. 16, No. 2, pp. 439-457.

Sironi, A. (2003), "Testing for Market Discipline in the European Banking Industry: Evidence from Subordinated Debt Issues", *Journal of Money, Credit, and Banking*, Vol. 35, No. 3, pp. 443-472.

Stiroh, K.J. (2004), "Diversification in Banking: Is Non-interest Income the Answer?", *Journal of Money, Credit, and Banking*, Vol. 36, No. 5, pp. 853-882.

_____ (2006a), "New Evidence on the Determinants of Bank Risk", *Journal of Financial Services Research*, Vol. 30, No. 3, pp. 237-263.

_____ (2006b), "A Portfolio View of Banking with Interest and Non-interest Activities", *Journal of Money, Credit, and Banking*, Vol. 38, No. 5, pp. 1351-1361.

Stiroh, K.J. and A. Rumble (2006), "The Dark Side of Diversification: The Case of US Financial Holding Companies", *Journal of Banking and Finance*, Vol. 30, No. 8, pp. 2131-2161.

Tett, G. (2008), "Leaders at wits' end as markets throw one tantrum after another", *Financial Times*, 11 October.

Van Wensveen, D. (2008), "Banks Prosper against the Odds: Why?", *De Economist*, Vol. 156, No. 3, pp 307-338.

Ward, J.H. (1963), "Hierarchical grouping to optimize objective function", *Journal of the American Statistical Association*, Vol. 58, No. 301, pp. 236-244.

Wehinger, G. (2008), "Lessons from the Financial Market Turmoil: Challenges Ahead for the Financial Industry and Policy Makers", *Financial Market Trends*, OECD, Paris.

World Bank/IMF (2005), *Financial Sector Assessment: A Handbook*, jointly published by the World Bank and the International Monetary Fund, Washington, D.C.

LIST OF ABBREVIATIONS

BCBS	Basel Committee on Banking Supervision
BIS	Bank for International Settlements
CDO	Collateralised debt obligation
CDS	Credit default swap
CEBS	Committee of European Banking Supervisors
CIR	Cost-to-income ratio
CNI	Central Network Institutions
CRD	Capital Requirements Directive
EBA	European Banking Authority
FSC	Financial Stability Contribution
NFSR	Net stable funding ratio
OTC	Over-the-counter
RoA	Return on assets
RoE	Return on equity
RWA	Risk-weighted assets
SHV	Shareholder-value
SIFI	Systemically important financial institution
SIVs	Structured investment vehicle
SPV	Special purpose vehicle
TBTF	Too-big-to-fail
XBRL	eXtensible Business Reporting Language

APPENDIX I.
LIST OF VARIABLES COLLECTED

No.	Variable	Coverage	No.	Variable	Coverage
1	Country (headquarter location)	100%	32	Share price (daily return)	67%
2	Reporting currency	100%	33	Share price (st. dev. daily return)	67%
3	Accounting method	100%	34	Share price (market Beta)	67%
4	Annual report (pages)	100%	35	Share price (interest Beta)	67%
5	Accounting date (end of year)	100%	36	Employees (FTEs)	65%
6	Annual Report (approval date)	96%	37	Employees (FTEs - Male)	21%
7	Accounting firm	100%	38	Employees (FTEs - Female)	21%
8	Total accounting fee	90%	39	Employees (headcount)	56%
9	Total non-audit fee	88%	40	Employees (headcount - Male)	25%
10	Ownership (SHV/STV)	100%	41	Employees (headcount - Female)	25%
11	Ownership (cooperative, savings...)	100%	42	Employees (domestic)	69%
12	Public ownership (%)	100%	43	Employees (other EU27 countries)	38%
13	Public ownership (domestic %)	100%	44	Employees (outside EU27)	69%
14	Public ownership (domestic name)	31%	45	Employees (training hours)	29%
15	Public ownership (other EU27 %)	100%	46	Employees (training employees)	19%
16	Public ownership (other EU27 name)	7%	47	Branches (total)	92%
17	Public ownership (outside EU27 %)	100%	48	Branches (domestic)	83%
18	Public ownership (outside EU27 name)	8%	49	Branches (other EU27 countries)	47%
19	Largest shareholder (% ownership)	90%	50	Branches (outside EU27)	76%
20	Largest shareholder (name)	94%	51	ATMs (total)	31%
21	Block holder ownership (>5%)	87%	52	ATMs (domestic)	25%
22	Block holder ownership (>3%)	63%	53	ATMs (other EU27 countries)	14%
23	Listed (YES/NO)	100%	54	ATMs (outside EU27)	11%
24	Ordinary shares (outstanding)	72%	55	Assets (total)	100%
25	Ordinary shares (traded)	66%	56	Assets (domestic)	56%
26	Market capitalisation	72%	57	Cash (and balances with central banks)	100%
27	Value of traded shares	66%	58	Assets (central bank)	60%
28	Gross dividend	72%	59	Loans to banks (total)	100%
29	Share price (year end)	72%	60	Loans to banks (nostro accounts / on demand)	27%
30	Share price (average)	67%	61	Loans to banks (loan loss provision)	58%
31	Share price (standard deviation)	67%	62	Loans to customers (total)	96%

No.	Variable	Coverage	No.	Variable	Coverage
63	Loans to customers (public sector)	28%	94	CDS spread (subordinated, volatility)	62%
64	Loans to customers (mortgage loans)	51%	95	Income (total)	100%
65	Loans to customers (loan loss provision)	69%	96	Income (interest - net)	100%
66	Loans to customers (collective impairment)	22%	97	Income (interest - income)	94%
67	Loans to customers (specific impairment)	22%	98	Income (interest - expenses)	94%
68	Intangible assets	100%	99	Income (non-interest)	100%
69	Goodwill	100%	100	Income (commissions - net)	100%
70	Reverse repurchase agreements	89%	101	Income (commissions - income)	91%
71	Liabilities (total)	100%	102	Income (commissions - expenses)	91%
72	Liabilities (domestic)	27%	103	Income (trading - net)	98%
73	Liabilities (banks incl. central banks)	96%	104	Income (dividend)	38%
74	Deposits (banks)	72%	105	Income (insurance - net)	74%
75	Deposits (domestic banks)	27%	106	Income (insurance - income)	72%
76	Deposits (central banks)	44%	107	Income (insurance - expenses)	72%
77	Deposits (banks - demand)	46%	108	Income (other)	94%
78	Deposits (banks - term)	43%	109	Expenses (operating - total)	100%
79	Liabilities (customers)	96%	110	Expenses (operating - administrative)	99%
80	Deposits (customers)	80%	111	Expenses (operating - personal)	93%
81	Deposits (domestic customers)	42%	112	Expenses (operating - personal training)	27%
82	Deposits (customers - term and time deposits)	54%	113	Expenses (operating - other)	93%
83	Deposits (customers - current accounts and demand)	46%	114	Expenses (operating - depreciations)	99%
84	Deposits (customers - savings)	55%	115	Profit (before tax)	100%
85	Repurchase agreements (liabilities)	92%	116	Income tax	100%
86	Short-selling position (total)	63%	117	Profit (after tax)	100%
87	Short-selling position (equity)	7%	118	Risk-weighted assets (total)	87%
88	Short-selling position (debt)	7%	119	Risk-weighted assets (off balance sheet)	16%
89	CDS spread (senior, year end)	69%	120	Risk-weighted assets (credit risk)	36%
90	CDS spread (senior, average)	69%	121	Risk-weighted assets (market risk)	36%
91	CDS spread (senior, volatility)	69%	122	Risk-weighted assets (operational risk)	30%
92	CDS spread (subordinated, year end)	62%	123	Risk-weighted assets (business risk)	10%
93	CDS spread (subordinated, average)	62%	124	Capital (regulatory capital)	93%
			125	Capital (tier I - total)	93%

No.	Variable	Coverage	No.	Variable	Coverage
126	Capital (tier I - core)	27%	152	Derivatives (total - nominal value)	22%
127	Capital (tier I - hybrid)	56%	153	Derivatives (total - notional value)	55%
128	Capital (tier II - total)	76%	154	Derivatives (total - notional value - receive)	14%
129	Capital (tier II - subordinated liabilities)	27%	155	Derivatives (total - notional value - deliver)	14%
130	Capital (tier II - hybrid)	15%	156	Derivatives (total - fair value - positive)	95%
131	Capital (tier III - total)	76%	157	Derivatives (total - fair value - negative)	95%
132	Capital (equity - total)	100%	158	Derivatives (interest - nominal value)	22%
133	Capital (equity - shareholders)	100%	159	Derivatives (interest - notional value)	55%
134	Capital (equity - minority interest)	100%	160	Derivatives (interest - notional value - receive)	14%
135	Capital (equity - special securities)	100%	161	Derivatives (interest - notional value - deliver)	14%
136	Capital (equity - hybrid)	100%	162	Derivatives (interest - fair value - positive)	92%
137	Capital (equity - subordinated liabilities)	100%	163	Derivatives (interest - fair value - negative)	92%
138	Capital (equity - hybrid)	100%	164	Derivatives (currency - nominal value)	22%
139	Capital (tangible common equity)	100%	165	Derivatives (currency - notional value)	55%
140	Capital (common equity)	100%	166	Derivatives (currency - notional value - receive)	14%
141	Capital (common stock)	96%	167	Derivatives (currency - notional value - deliver)	14%
142	Capital (additional paid-in capital)	96%	168	Derivatives (currency - fair value - positive)	92%
143	Capital (retained earnings)	100%	169	Derivatives (currency - fair value - negative)	92%
144	Capital (treasury shares)	98%	170	Derivatives (equity - nominal value)	22%
145	Capital (non-recognised losses)	99%	171	Derivatives (equity - notional value)	55%
146	Capital (subscribed capital - issuance)	100%	172	Derivatives (equity - notional value - receive)	14%
147	Capital (non-common equity - issuance)	100%	173	Derivatives (equity - notional value - deliver)	14%
148	Rating (DBRS)	19%	174	Derivatives (equity - fair value - positive)	92%
149	Rating (Fitch)	69%	175	Derivatives (equity - fair value - negative)	92%
150	Rating (Moody's)	80%	176	Derivatives (credit - nominal value)	22%
151	Rating (S&P)	79%	177	Derivatives (credit - notional value)	55%
			178	Derivatives (credit - notional value - receive)	18%

No.	Variable	Coverage	No.	Variable	Coverage
179	Derivatives (credit - notional value - deliver)	18%	191	Derivatives (hedging - notional value)	30%
180	Derivatives (credit - fair value - positive)	93%	192	Derivatives (hedging - fair value - positive)	78%
181	Derivatives (credit - fair value - negative)	92%	193	Derivatives (hedging - fair value - negative)	78%
182	Derivatives (FX - nominal value)	15%	194	Derivatives (trading - notional value - receive)	11%
183	Derivatives (FX - notional value)	27%	195	Derivatives (trading - notional value - deliver)	11%
184	Derivatives (FX - fair value - positive)	37%	196	Derivatives (trading - fair value - positive)	79%
185	Derivatives (FX - fair value - negative)	37%	197	Derivatives (trading - fair value - negative)	78%
186	Derivatives (OTC - nominal value)	19%	198	Asset-backed securities (total)	34%
187	Derivatives (OTC - notional value)	22%	199	Asset-backed securities (impaired)	11%
188	Derivatives (OTC - fair value - positive)	37%	200	Asset-backed securities (CDOs)	22%
189	Derivatives (OTC - fair value - negative)	37%	201	Asset-backed securities (RMBSs)	21%
190	Derivatives (hedging - nominal value)	13%	202	Asset-backed securities (CMBSs)	19%

APPENDIX II. CALCULATION OF Z-SCORE

The Z-score used in the study is the one derived in Boyd & Runkle (1993), which is a simple indicator of the risk of failure or the distance to default. To derive the measure, it is assumed that default occurs when the one-time losses of bank j in year t exceed its equity, or when

$$\pi_{jt} + E_{jt} < 0. \tag{A1}$$

Then, assuming that the bank's return on total assets (RoA), or π_{jt}/TA_{jt}, is normally distributed around the mean μ_j, and standard deviation σ_j, the probability of failure is given as

$$pr(\pi_{jt} < -E_{jt}) = pr(\pi_{jt}/TA_{jt} < -E_{jt}/TA_{jt}) = \int_{-\infty}^{D_{jt}} \phi(r)dr, \tag{A2}$$

where ϕ represents the standard normal distribution, r is the standardised return on assets and D is the default boundary that separates a healthy bank from an unhealthy one, described as the normalised equity ratio:

$$D_{jt} = \frac{-(E_{jt}/TA_{jt}) - \mu_j}{\sigma_j}, \tag{A3}$$

Note that a greater D implies a greater probability of default and, therefore, a greater risk for the bank. The average and standard deviation calculations were obtained using available data for the years 2006-09.

Since D admits negative values in most cases, the Z-score is set to be represented as a positive number, or as

$$Z_{jt} = -D_{jt}. \tag{A4}$$

This implies that a greater Z-value implies a lower probability of default.

APPENDIX III. RECENT DEVELOPMENTS IN SAMPLED BANKS

Bank: Dexia	Country: Belgium

Activities. The listed financial group Dexia SA was created in 1996 by the merger of three financial groups specialised in providing financial services to local governments in Belgium, France and Luxembourg. Insurance and retail activities, mostly concentrated in Belgium and Turkey, are more secondary. Due to its lower reliance on customer deposits and its lack of trading activity, in particular in the derivatives market, the bank is categorised as a wholesale bank in the cluster analysis. There is some evidence, however, that Dexia has been moving closer to retail banking in 2009.

State aid. Dexia received a large package of state aid measures from the Belgian, French and Luxembourg governments during the crisis.[45] This package, provided in November 2008, contained a capital injection of €6 billion, a guarantee on liabilities of up to €150 billion (reduced to €100 billion in November 2009) and a guarantee of $16.6 billion (€13 billion) on impaired assets. In addition, the bank received emergency liquidity support from central banks, e.g. the Belgium Central Bank and the US Federal Reserve.[46]

Restructuring. In line with the provisions stated in the Commission's approval of state aid in February 2010, Dexia has to focus more on retail banking activities in its countries of origin by reducing public-sector lending, bond portfolio, market activities and disengaging from trading activities.

Bank: KBC Group	Country: Belgium

Activities. The listed financial group KBC provides primarily banking and insurance services to retail customers and SMEs in Belgium and Eastern Europe.

State aid. During the crisis, the banking group was recapitalised twice (i.e. in December 2008 and June 2009) by the Belgium federal- and Flemish regional government for a total

---

[45] Commission Decision of 26 February 2010 on State aid C 9/09 (ex NN 49/08, NN 50/08 and NN 45/08) implemented by the Kingdom of Belgium, the French Republic and the Grand Duchy of Luxembourg for Dexia SA, *Official Journal* L274, 19 October 2010 (http://eur-lex.europa.eu/LexUriServ/LexUriServ.do?uri=OJ:L:2010:274:0054:0102:EN:PDF).

[46] Dexia borrowed up to $31.5 billion (€25 billion) of the FED's discount window. See Bloomberg, "Dexia Drew Most From Discount Window in Record Week in 2008", Bradley Keoun, Bloomberg, 31 March 2011 (http://www.bloomberg.com/news/2011-03-31/belgium-s-dexia-drew-most-from-discount-window-during-record-week-in-2008.html).

amount of €7 billion. In addition, the government took over part of the risk on several collateralised debt obligation (CDO) portfolios of a total notional value of €20 billion.[47]

Restructuring. In line with the provisions of the Commission's approval of state aid, KBC has to sell or cease a significant number of businesses, particularly non-core business. Among the activities to be sold are interests in Belgian Centea Bank and Fidea Insurance with the aim of enhancing competition.

Bank: BayernLB	Country: Germany

Activities. The second largest German Landesbank, BayernLB provides financing for companies located in Bavaria, the Bavarian municipalities and the Bavarian state, the latter of which is its majority owner. Furthermore, the bank acts as the central network institution for the local savings banks, which in turn hold a minority stake in the bank.

State aid. In order to continue operating, in December 2008 BayernLB obtained aid from the Bavarian state in the form of a capital injection of €10 billion and a risk shield for its asset-backed securities of €4.8 billion. In addition to the measures taken by the Bavarian state, the federal Financial Market Stabilisation Fund (SoFFin) provided €15 billion guarantees. The subsidiary Hypo Group Alpe Adria (HGAA) also received €0.9 billion of capital injection by the Austrian government.[48] This first capital injection by the Austrian government and BayernLB was insufficient; in December 2009 HGAA was fully acquired by the Austrian government.[49]

Restructuring. Ahead of a decision about its restructuring plan by the European Commission and the reform of the Landesbank sector, BayernLB sold 25.2% of its shares in Landesbank SaarLB to the State of Saarland.[50,51] Furthermore, BayernLB and WestLB have been in negotiations at the end of 2010 about the feasibility of a merger between the two banks.[52]

---

[47] Commission Decision of 18 November 2009 on the State aid C 18/09 (ex N 360/09) implemented by Belgium for KBC, *Official Journal* L188, 21 July 2010 (http://eur-lex.europa.eu/LexUriServ/LexUriServ.do?uri=OJ:L:2010:188:0024:0051:EN:PDF).

[48] State aid C 16/09 (ex N 254/09) and N 698/09 — BayernLB, Germany, and Hypo Group Alpe Adria, Austria, *Official Journal* C85, 31 March 2010 (http://eur-lex.europa.eu/LexUriServ/LexUriServ.do?uri=OJ:C:2010:085:0021:0029:EN:PDF).

[49] BayernLB tries to recover losses of the acquisition of HGAA from two former members of the supervisory board who would have failed to call a decisive supervisory board meeting. See "BayernLB to seek damages", *Financial Times*, 16 March 2011, p. 17 (http://presscuttings.ft.com/presscuttings/s/3/viewPdf/45580040).

[50] BayernLB, "The Saarland to purchase BayernLB's shares of SaarLB", press release, 21 December 2009 (http://www.bayernlb.de/internet/ln/ar/sc/Internet/en/Downloads/0100_Corporate Center/1323Presse_Politik/Pressemeldungen/2009/12Dec/21122009_SaarLB-e.pdf).

[51] BayernLB's remaining 49.9% of the shares will most probably be transferred in the upcoming years (http://www.bayernlb.de/internet/ln/ar/sc/Internet/en/Downloads/0100_CorporateCenter/1323Presse_Politik/Pressemeldungen/2009/12Dec/21122009_SaarLB-e.pdf).

[52] BayernLB, "BayernLB discontinues merger talks with WestLB", press release, 4 November 2010, BayernLB (http://www.bayernlb.de/internet/ln/ar/sc/Internet/en/Downloads/

Bank: Commerzbank	Country: Germany
Activities. Commerzbank became the second largest private credit institution in Germany following the acquisition of Dresdner Bank in May 2009. The listed banking group mainly focuses on commercial banking, serving the retail clients and small- and medium-sized corporations (SMEs) in Germany as well as through its affiliates in Central and Eastern Europe. In addition, Commerzbank explores substantial investment banking activities. However, it was the scale of interbank activities that qualified Commerzbank to be identified as a wholesale bank in the cluster analysis for the years 2006 to 2008. In 2009, the acquisition of Dresdner has led to a substantial jump in the bank's trading activities and in particular derivative transactions, resulting in the re-categorisation of the bank as an investment bank in the cluster analysis.	
State aid. During the financial crisis, Commerzbank was recapitalised twice, once in December 2008 and again in May 2009, for a total amount of €18.2 billion and received guarantees on issued bearer bonds of up to €15 billion. The capital problems of Commerzbank were mainly derived from major losses on ABS portfolio acquired by the takeover of Dresdner. In April 2011, the bank announced its plans to repay the silent participation of €16.2 billion by issuing €11 billion new shares, of which a quarter will be acquired by the government. The remaining €5.2 billion will be repaid by excess regulatory capital by 2014 at the latest.[53]	
Restructuring. In line with the provisions of the Commission's approval of state aid, Commerzbank is forced to sell part of its subsidiaries engaging primarily in private banking before the beginning of 2012.[54] In addition, the bank is to divest its interests in the commercial real estate banking and public finance business of Eurohypo AG by December 2014. Meanwhile it has to shrink the public finance business portfolio by more than a third before the beginning of 2013.[55] In addition, the bank also has to reduce its market presence in investment banking and in Central and Eastern Europe.[56]	

0100_CorporateCenter/1323Presse_Politik/Pressemeldungen/2010/11November/04112010-WestLB-e.pdf).

[53] Commerzbank, "Commerzbank intends to largely reduce silent participations of SoFFin", press release, 6 April 2011 (https://www.commerzbank.de/en/hauptnavigation/aktionaere/service/archive/ir-nachrichten_1/2011_6/ir_nachrichten_detail_11_3096.html).

[54] Commerzbank will have to sell its shareholdings in Kleinwort Benson Private Bank Limited and Kleinwort Benson, (Channel Islands) Holdings Limited, United Kingdom (including the Channel Islands); Dresdner Van Moer Courtens S.A., Belgium; Dresdner VPV NV, the Netherlands; Privatinvest Bank AG, Austria; Reuschel & Co. Kommanditgesellschaft, Germany; and Allianz Dresdner Bauspar AG, Germany.

[55] The public finance business portfolio of Commerzbank must be reduced from around €160 billion mid-year 2009 to around €100 billion by December 2012.

[56] State aid N 244/2009 – Commerzbank – Germany, C(2009) 3708 final, 7 May 2009 (http://ec.europa.eu/competition/state_aid/cases/231053/231053_959312_23_1.pdf).

Bank: Deutsche Bank	Country: Germany

Activities. The listed financial group Deutsche Bank offers a broad range of banking services to private and corporate clients both internationally and in Germany. In addition, the bank has substantial investment banking activities including e.g. M&A advisory and trading. The bank, for instance, was the fourth-largest global issuer of, for example, Collateralised Debt Obligations (CDOs) at the time the US housing bubble burst.[57]

Crisis. Although Deutsche Bank reported lower profitability, the bank did not receive state aid during the crisis and issued €2.2 billion new shares in 2009.[58] In the aftermath of the crisis, the bank extended its German retail network by acquiring Deutsche Postbank AG while further strengthening its capital position with the issuance of new shares worth €10.2 billion in October 2010.[59]

Legal. Since the outbreak of the financial crisis, the group received several claims from customers for providing insufficient and wrong information on the inherent risks of its financial products. In 2008 and 2009, the group repurchased products from private investors which led to additional costs of approximately €300 million for the group, of which about €100 million was for a settlement in the US. The US Government has, for instance, charged $1 billion (€0.7 billion) to Deutsche Bank and its subsidiary MortgageIT for misleading the US authorities to qualify for the Federal Housing Administration (FHA) insurance scheme, which guarantees mortgage loans.[60] In addition, the bank is subject to industry-wide investigations of US, Japan and UK regulators on the manipulation of the LIBOR benchmark interest rate[61] and the European Commission on the clearing and pricing information in the CDS market.[62]

Bank: DZ Bank	Country: Germany

Activities. DZ Bank AG is the central network institution for most local cooperative banks in Germany, engaging primarily in interbank activities with its network. In addition, the bank functions as a corporate bank for medium- and large-sized companies and institutional investors. Although the bank did not receive any state aid, it increased

---

[57] For more information, see Reuters, Global ABS CDO issuance 2006 and 2007, Reuters, 20 April 2010 (http://graphics.thomsonreuters.com/10/04/GLB_GCDOV0410.gif).

[58] Deutsche Bank noted a net loss in 2008 and lower profits in 2009 and 2010. The loss in 2008 was mainly due to a net loss of €10 billion on assets/liabilities at fair value i.e. losses in credit trading, equity derivative and equity proprietary trading.

[59] Deutsche Bank, "Deutsche Bank successfully completes capital increase", press release, 6 October 2010 (http://www.db.com/ir/en/download/IR-Release_2010_10_06.pdf).

[60] Financial Times, "Deutsche accused of lying over US mortgages", Patrick Jenkins, 3 May 2011 (http://www.ft.com/cms/s/0/a1828f30-7592-11e0-8492-00144feabdc0.html#axzz1LIiN5zY0).

[61] Financial Times, "Big banks investigated over Libor", Brooke Masters, Patrick Jenkins and Justin Baer, 15 March 2011 (http://www.ft.com/cms/s/0/ab563882-4f08-11e0-9c25-00144feab49a.html#axzz1LIiN5zY0).

[62] European Commission, "Antitrust: Commission probes Credit Default Swaps market", 29 April 2011 (http://europa.eu/rapid/pressReleasesAction.do?reference=IP/11/509&format=HTML&aged=0&language=EN&guiLanguage=en).

its capital by issuing €400 million of new shares to other cooperatives in the network at the end of 2009.[63]

Merger. In the beginning of 2009, the DZ Bank and WGZ Bank, the central network institution for the rest of Germany's cooperative banks, entered into negotiations to merge their networks. The talks were officially suspended because of the turmoil in the financial markets.[64]

Bank: Hypo Real Estate Holding	Country: Germany

Activities. Commercial real estate and public sector financer Hypo Real Estate Holding AG was established in October 2003, as a spin-off of the HVB Group. The size of the bank's activities grew substantially by the takeover of Irish public sector financer DEPFA Bank just prior to the onset of the financial crisis in 2007. The group mainly funds its activities via short-term interbank debt and debt securities, e.g. mortgage and public sector bonds. The bank's scale of interbank operations, including loans, is the reason that it was categorised as a wholesale bank in the cluster analysis.

State aid. Hypo Real Estate encountered its first immediate financial problems in October 2008, when it was not able to raise sufficient short-term funding to continue its operations. Since then, the bank benefited from approximately €7.9 billion of capital injections, up to €145 billion of state guarantees and undisclosed amounts of liquidity by central banks. Since October 2009, the bank is fully owned by the German federal government. In September 2010 a 'bad bank' was formed, which received up to €200 billion of toxic and non-strategic assets to make Deutsche Pfandbriefbank, the 'good bank', more viable.

Restructuring. Following the proposed restructuring plan made to the European Commission under state aid procedures, Hypo Real Estate had to restructure its business, reducing the size of its activities in real estate and public sector finance, shrinking assets by almost 75% to €110-120 billion at the end of 2010. This should reduce the dependency of short-term financing of the bank. Despite the thorough restructuring, the European Commission still has doubts about the viability of Hypo Real Estate. Therefore the European Commission only gave temporal approval to the state aid and extended the scope of the proceedings in September 2010.[65]

---

[63] DZ Bank, "DZ BANK successfully completes capital increase", press release, 2 November 2009 (http://www.dzbank.com/components/getirdl.php?id=193).

[64] DZ Bank, "DZ BANK and WGZ BANK decide not to pursue their merger talks further for the time being", press release, 1 April 2009 (http://www.dzbank.com/components/getirdl.php?id=127).

[65] State aid C 15/09 (ex N 196/09) and N 380/10 — Extension of scope of formal investigation procedure, winding-up institution, additional SoFFin guarantees for HRE: Hypo Real Estate, *Official Journal*, 2010/C 300/06, 6 November 2010 (http://eur-lex.europa.eu/LexUriServ/LexUriServ.do?uri=OJ:C:2010:300:0006:0016:EN:PDF).

Bank: Landesbank Baden-Württemberg	Country: Germany

Activities. Landesbank Baden-Württemberg (LBBW) primarily functions as a central network institution for the savings banks in Baden-Württemberg, Saxony (since 2008) and Rhineland Palatinate (since 2005). As more secondary functions, the bank engages in real estate financing as well as providing retail activities to SMEs and larger corporations. Despite an increasing share of trading activities in 2008 and 2009, the bank is nevertheless categorised as a wholesale bank in the cluster analysis due to the scale of its interbank activities.

State aid. LBBW received in June 2009 a capital injection of €5 billion by its shareholders, including all public entities and governments, after facing large losses and higher capital requirements.[66] In addition, German states took two impaired asset relief measures, totalling €12.7 billion of guarantees on structured securities. The majority of the guarantees (€8.8 billion) were backing the portfolio acquired from the SachsenLB, part of the 2008 take-over deal.[67,68]

Restructuring. In line with the agreement struck with the European Commission under state aid procedures, LBBW will have to restructure its business model to align it more closely with a more retail services focus, diminishing its capital markets and proprietary trading activities.

Bank: WestLB	Country: Germany

Activities. Westdeutsche Landesbank (WestLB) is a central network institution for the saving banks of German State North Rhine-Westphalia. Despite its main function, WestLB carries out commercial and investment banking operations. The bank's increasing engagement in trading activities, especially in derivative transactions, is the main driving force behind its categorisation as an investment bank and not a wholesale bank in the cluster analysis.

State aid. During the crisis, the bank's exposures to structured finance products and its reliance on short-term funding were its main weaknesses. In mid-2007, the bank was unable to rollover the funding for its structured finance assets. In order to solve the problem, the bank's portfolio of toxic assets, representing a nominal value of €85.1 billion, was ring-fenced in a so-called 'bad bank'. In 2009, WestLB also received a capital injection of €7 billion from the German government.[69]

---

[66] All shareholders contributed to the capital injection in proportion to their shareholdings: Baden-Württemberg state (35.5%), Stuttgart (19%), savings banks associations of Baden-Württemberg (41%) and the Landeskreditbank Baden-Württemberg (almost 5%).

[67] Commission Decision of 15 December 2009 on State aid C 17/09 (ex N 265/09) by Germany for the restructuring of Landesbank Baden-Württemberg, *Official Journal* L 188, 21 July 2010 (http://eur-lex.europa.eu/LexUriServ/LexUriServ.do?uri=OJ:L:2010:188:0001:0023:EN:PDF).

[68] SachsenLB, "Takeover of Sachsen LB complete", press release, 7 March 2008 (http://www.lbbw.de/lbbwde/1000011757-s1048-en.html).

[69] STATE AID — GERMANY State aid C 40/09 (ex N 555/09) Extension of formal investigation procedure, WestLB AG Invitation to submit comments pursuant to Article 108(2) TFEU, *Official*

Restructuring. In May 2009, the bank faced a restructuring plan in order to stop proprietary trading, halving its total assets and bringing its core areas of business into focus. But in February 2010, the European Commission required additional restructuring measures after it found that the amount of the initial capital injection support was understated by €3.4 billion. The measures proposed by the bank in February 2011 contain a splitting-up of the bank into four parts and shrinking the assets by an extra third.[70] Meanwhile WestLB remains in discussion with BayernLB for an eventual merger.[71]

Bank: Danske Bank	Country: Denmark

Activities. Danske Bank Group provides retail banking services in Scandinavia, the Baltics and (Northern) Ireland. In recent years, the listed bank has expanded into pension, life-insurance, asset management and substantial capital markets activities. However, the bank is categorised as a wholesale bank due to the scale of its interbank activities, especially interbank loans that represent nearly 40% of the balance sheet.

Growth. The financial crisis ended a decade-long series of major acquisitions for the bank, which started in 1997 with the acquisition of Enskilda in Sweden (1997) and continued with the acquisition of Focus Bank in Norway (1999), National Irish Bank in Ireland and Northern Bank in Northern Ireland (2005), and, most recently, Sampo Bank in Finland (2007).[72]

State aid. The economic slowdown and falling property prices in Denmark and Ireland led to higher impairment charges and lower profits in the period 2007 to 2009. In consequence, the bank had to seek a capital injection of 26 billion Danish krona (approximately €3.5 billion) from the Danish government in May 2009, which was provided as hybrid capital.[73] The state aid was repaid in March 2011 by the issuance of 20 billion Danish krona (approximately €2.7 billion) worth of new shares.[74] Danske also

---

Journal, 2011/C 23/07, 25 January (http://eur-lex.europa.eu/LexUriServ/LexUriServ.do?uri=OJ:C:2011:023:0009:0032:EN:PDF).

[70] WestLB, "Restructuring Plan Submitted to the European Commission within the Agreed Timeframe", press release, 16 February 2011 (http://www.westlb.de/cms/sitecontent/westlb/westlb_de/en/wlb/ui/news/newscontainer/news_2011/meldung.standard.gid-N2FkNDZmMzU4OWFmYTIyMWM3N2Q2N2Q0YmU1NmI0OGU_.html).

[71] WestLB, "WestLB Regrets Premature Break-Off of Merger Talks by BayernLB", press release, 4 November 2010 (http://www.westlb.de/cms/sitecontent/westlb/westlb_de/en/wlb/ui/news/newscontainer/news_2010/eigen.standard.gid-N2FkNDZmMzU4OWFmYTIyMWM3N2Q2N2Q0YmU1NmI0OGU_.html).

[72] Danske Bank Group, "The Group", 2011 (http://www.danskebank.com/en-uk/about-us/History/Pages/Group.aspx).

[73] Danmarks Nationalbank, Financial stability report 2010, 2010.

[74] Danske Bank Group, "Danske Bank sets terms for rights offering and publishes prospectus", press release, 14 March 2011 (http://www.danskebank.com/en-uk/press/News/Press-releases-and-company-announcements/Company%20announcement/Group/Pages/ca14032011.aspx).

reduced its activities in Ireland and changed the organisational structure by appointing a special risk officer on the executive committee.[75,76]

Bank: Banco Bilbao Vizcaya Argentaria	Country: Spain

Activities. The listed financial group Banco Bilbao Vizcaya Argentaria S.A. (BBVA) provides financial services to households, SMEs, large corporations, governments and local authorities in Spain, Portugal, Latin America and the United States. In addition to its primary retail activities, BBVA also operates asset management, capital markets and insurance arms.

Crisis. The impact of the financial crisis on BBVA has been relatively limited, absorbed mainly through lower profits. Nevertheless, the bank issued preference shares, mandatory convertible bonds and subordinated debt and sold tangible assets to raise its capital level and expand activities.[77]

Expansion. After a period of no acquisitions during the crisis, BBVA raised its equity stake in Chinese Citic Bank to 15% in 2009, and acquired Guaranty Bank assets and liabilities from FDIC in the US and public financer Banco de Crédito Local de España in Spain. In 2010, BBVA acquired almost 25% of Garanti Bank in Turkey for €4.2 billion.[78]

Bank: Banco Santander	Country: Spain

Activities. The Spanish financial group Banco Santander is primarily engaged in retail and commercial banking. In addition, Santander undertakes asset management, wholesale banking and insurance activities. Besides in Spain, the listed bank has significant presence within the EU (including affiliates in Germany, Italy, Portugal and UK), Latin America (Brazil, Chile and Mexico), and the United States.[79] Due to a low proportion of trading and interbank activities, which are the main characteristics of

---

[75] National Irish Bank, "National Irish Bank restructures, confirms commitment to Ireland", press release, 7 December 2009 (http://www.nationalirishbank.ie/en-ie/About-National-Irish-Bank/Press/Press-releases/2009/Pages/PressReleaseChangesToYourBank.aspx).

[76] Danske Bank Group, "Danske Bank adjusts organisation and appoints Chief Risk Officer", press release, 16 December 2009 (http://www.danskebank.com/en-uk/press/News/Press-releases-and-company-announcements/Company%20announcement/Group/Pages/ca16122009.aspx.

[77] In 2009 BBVA sold 948 properties, mostly offices in Spain, to Tree Inversiones Inmobiliarias under a long term sale and lease-back agreement. The bank made a gross capital gain of €0.8 billion. Banco Bilbao Vizcaya Argentaria, "BBVA obtains €1,154 million from the sale of 948 properties", press release, 25 September 2009 (http://press.bbva.com/latest-contents/press-releases/spain/bbva-obtains-1-154-million-from-the-sale-of-948-properties(9882-22-101-c-44492).html).

[78] Banco Bilbao Vizcaya Argentaria, "BBVA to acquire a 24.9% stake in Garanti, Turkey's leading bank", press release, 2 November 2010 (http://press.bbva.com/bbva-to-acquire-a-24-9-stake-in-garanti-turkeys-leading-bank.html).

[79] Banco Santander S.A., "Banco Santander Annual Report 2009", 2010.

investment and wholesale banks, respectively, the bank is categorised as a retail bank in the cluster analysis.

Crisis. Santander has not received any direct state aid during the financial crisis, continuing to improve its market position in retail and commercial banking activities in Europe, with autonomous growth and acquisition of troubled banks. The recent acquisitions include the UK branch networks of Bradford & Bingley and part of the Royal Bank of Scotland in 2008 and 2010[80]; retail banking business of Swedish SEB in Germany;[81] and around 70% of Bank Zachodni's retail banking network WBK in Poland.[82]

Expansion. Just before the crisis erupted, Santander bought parts of ABN Amro, of which it kept the Latin American business (Banco Real) and resold the Italian Antonveneta bank.[83] Although Santander's acquisitions are usually financed by own equity and retained earnings, for the takeover of ABN Amro the bank issued €7 billion of mandatory convertible bonds and sold tangible assets and divested some of the non-core investments.

Bank: BNP Paribas	Country: France

Activities. The French listed financial group BNP Paribas is present in several key EU markets. In addition to France and Italy, since the acquisition of Fortis Bank and BGL in 2009, the bank has a substantial presence in Belgium and Luxembourg. Besides its retail, corporate lending and real estate financing activities, the bank's primary activity lies in trading, especially in the capital markets, and derivative transactions.

Crisis. The group was one of the first banks to show signs of the eruption of a financial crisis when it froze three investment funds in August 2007.[84] Despite greater provisions due to increased risks, BNP Paribas managed to remain profitable during the financial

---

[80] Banco Santander S.A., "Santander agrees to acquire 318 RBS branches for EUR 1.99 billion", press release, 4 August 2010 (http://www.santander.com/csgs/BlobServer?blobtable=MungoBlobs&blobheader=application%2Fpdf&blobwhere=1265281592309&blobcol=urldata&blobkey=id&leng=en_GB).

[81] Banco Santander S.A., "Santander to acquire SEB's German retail banking business for EUR 555 million", press release, 12 July 2010 (http://www.santander.com/csgs/BlobServer?blobtable=MungoBlobs&blobheader=application%2Fpdf&blobwhere=1265280146183&blobcol=urldata&blobkey=id&leng=en_GB).

[82] Banco Santander, "Santander to acquire 70% of Bank Zachodni WBK of Poland from AIB for EUR 2.938 billion", press release, 10 September 2010 (http://www.santander.com/csgs/BlobServer?blobtable=MungoBlobs&blobheader=application%2Fpdf&blobwhere=1265283104170&blobcol=urldata&blobkey=id&leng=en_GB).

[83] Banco Santander sold Antonveneta Bank for €2.4 billion more to Monte dei Paschi di Siena.

[84] Financial Times, "BNP Paribas investment funds hit by volatility", Anuj Gangahar and Adam Jones, 9 August 2007 (http://www.ft.com/cms/s/0/9a4cabc4-464d-11dc-a3be-0000779fd2ac.html#axzz1LIiN5zY0.

turmoil. Like the other major French banks, the bank received capital injections provided by the French government.[85] All of the €5.1 billion of government aid received in exchange for non-voting shares in March 2009 (and under the condition of increased lending) were repaid by October of the same year, financed by the issuance of new common shares.

Bank: BPCE	Country: France

Activities. The BPCE group was created during the crisis in 2009 by the merger of Groupe Banque Populaire and Groupe Caisse d'Epargne. Prior to the merger, both banks served, among other functions, as central network institutions for their local cooperative and savings banks. The newly created group also suffered large losses from its investment arm, Natixis, and has received capital injections from the French government.[86,87]

Crisis. The merger of the bank between Natixis's owners Banque Populaire and Caisse d'Epargne was one of the conditions of the French government for providing additional state aid. In the first instance the banks injected own funds, partially obtained by state aid, in its investment bank Natixis, but this appeared to be insufficient. To obtain the necessary additional funds from the French government, the parent banks were forced to increase their grip on the investment bank by the merger.[88] However, Banque Populaire and Caisse d'Epargne also suffered from the crisis by higher risk costs and trading losses, e.g. Caisse Nationale des Caisses d'Epargne had one equity derivative position on which it lost €752 million.

State aid. In total BPCE received in two tranches a capital injection of €7.1 billion[89] from the French state (€2 billion in December 2008 and €5.1 billion in the first half of 2009). In exchange for €5.1 billion support, the French state received preference shares representing a share of 20%of the group. For the other €2 billion, the state received subordinated debt securities.[90] BPCE repaid €4.1 billion of the aid received from the French government.

---

[85] State aid N 29/2009 – French Republic Amendment to the capital-injection scheme for banks, C(2008) 597 final, 28 January 2009 (http://ec.europa.eu/competition/state_aid/cases/229327/229327_1015954_16_1.pdf).

[86] Between 2007 and 2009, Natixis reported a total negative net income of €5.6 billion.

[87] The investment bank Natixis was formed in 2006 by the merger of Banque Populaire's subsidiary Natexis and Caisse d'Epargne's subsidiary IXIS. Both banking groups held an equity stake of 35% in Natixis. The investment bank in its turn owns 20% of the regional Banque Populaires and Caisses d'Epargne banks.

[88] Financial Times, "Merger shakes up French mutuals", 13 July 2009 (http://www.ft.com/cms/s/0/f30f33e4-6fdb-11de-b835-00144feabdc0.html#axzz1HGPQQwLM).

[89] Due to the merger, BPCE had an additional capital requirement of €5 billion, because of accounting and prudential rules; e.g. Natixis was only proportionally consolidated for approximately 70% in the parent's figures whereas it is fully consolidated after the merger.

[90] State Aid N 249/2009 – French Republic Injection of capital into the institution to be created by the merger of the parent companies of the Caisse d'Épargne and Banque Populaire groups,

Bank: Crédit Agricole	Country: France

Activities. In addition to its retail activities in France, the Crédit Agricole group has substantial asset management, specialised finance (i.e. consumer finance, lease finance and factoring), corporate and investment banking and insurance activities. The listed group also owns subsidiaries in other EU member states (i.e. Italy, Greece, Spain and Portugal), the Middle East and Northern Africa. Despite these international and investment activities, due to the scale of its interbank activities, especially interbank loans representing over one-fifth of its total activities, the group is categorised as a wholesale bank in the cluster analysis.

State aid. The bank managed to remain profitable during the crisis and was able to offset its losses by rationalising costs, reducing capital market activities and halting acquisitions.[91] In July 2008, the group increased its capital by issuing €5.8 billion of new shares. In addition, and like the other major French banks, Crédit Agricole received a capital injection of €3 billion of capital contributing to Tier 1 in exchange for super-subordinated notes in December 2008.[92] The super-subordinated notes were repaid in full in October 2009 by issuing deeply subordinated debt on the financial markets. The French government also provided guarantees of up to €18.6 billion of collateralised loans used to issue additional debt to be used primarily for liquidity purposes.

Expansion. Crédit Agricole continued with its takeover activity in 2009 and onwards, with the acquisition of 23.4% (€1.1 billion) stakes in the Spanish Bankinter, an additional 35% (€0.6 billion) of French asset servicing provider CACEIS in 2009, and a 79.9% stake in the Italian Cassa di Risparmio della Spezi in 2011.[93]

Bank: Société Générale	Country: France

Activities. The listed financial group Société Générale undertakes primarily retail, corporate and investment banking activities. The group's retail network is present in France, Eastern Europe and Northern Africa. The corporate and investment bank activities are also spread around the globe, containing mainly trading activities and financial advisory services. Although its retail activities are sizeable, the bank primarily engages in trading activities, especially derivative transactions, which is the reason that the bank is categorised as an investment bank in the cluster analysis.

C(2009) 3835 final, 8 May 2009 (http://ec.europa.eu/competition/state_aid/cases/231081/231081_1014474_46_1.pdf).

[91] The financial crisis had a serious impact on the bank's investment arm and the Greek retail bank Emporiki.

[92] State aid N 29/2009 – French Republic Amendment to the capital-injection scheme for banks, C(2008) 597 final, 28 January 2009 (http://ec.europa.eu/competition/state_aid/cases/229327/229327_1015954_16_1.pdf).

[93] Crédit Agricole S.A., "Another major step forward in Crédit Agricole's expansion in Italy", press release, 11 January 2011 (http://www.credit-agricole.com/en/News/Press-releases/Financial-press-releases/Another-major-step-forward-in-Credit-Agricole-s-expansion-in-Italy).

Crisis. Société Générale reported lower but nevertheless positive net income figures during the financial turmoil.[94] The main losses have been related to financial instruments linked to US residential real estate. In addition in January 2008, the bank lost €4.9 billion due to the fraudulent activities of one of its traders, Jérôme Kerviel.[95] This loss was compensated by the issuance of €5.5 billion of new shares in February 2008.

State aid. Like the other major French banks, the group received a capital injection of €1.7 billion in exchange for preference shares.[96] The preference shares were repaid in November 2009 by issuing €4.8 billion new shares. Part of this amount was used to acquire the last 20% (€0.7 billion) of Crédit du Nord from Belgium's troubled bank Dexia.[97]

Bank: Intesa Sanpaolo Group	Country: Italy

Activities. Although the business and retail activities of the Intesa Sanpaolo Group are focused mainly in Italy, the bank also has a substantial presence in Central and Eastern Europe and Egypt. Retail clients and SMEs are the main source of income for the listed financial group. The Group was created in January 2007 through the merger of Banca Intesa and Sanpaolo IMI. In the last few years, Intesa Sanpaolo engaged in smaller takeovers to strengthen its core business, buying some of the branches of the Banca Monte dei Paschi di Siena in December 2009 and buying a majority stake in the Banca Monte Parma in October 2010.

Crisis. The Intesa Sanpaolo Group was hit relatively hard by the financial turmoil, which resulted in significant lower commission and trading income and higher impairments on equity and intangibles in 2008 and 2009. To increase its capital level and lending capacity, Intesa Sanpaolo issued hybrid capital instruments and sold non-core assets. In December 2009, the securities service business was sold for €1.8 billion to State Street Corporation. [98,99] In March 2009, Intesa Sanpaolo announced it would start procedures to receive a

---

[94] The net income of Société Générale dropped in 2007 and stayed at a lower level for three consecutive years 2007-10.

[95] Financial Times, "Kerviel found guilty in SocGen scandal", Scheherazade Daneshkhu, Financial Times, 5 October 2010 (http://www.ft.com/cms/s/0/bd166528-d05b-11df-afe1-00144feabdc0.html#axzz1HKuk3rbB).

[96] State aid N 29/2009 – French Republic Amendment to the capital-injection scheme for banks, C(2008) 597 final, 28 January 2009 (http://ec.europa.eu/competition/state_aid/cases/229327/229327_1015954_16_1.pdf).

[97] Société Générale, "Société Générale and Dexia complete the Crédit du Nord transaction", press release, 11 December 2009 (http://phx.corporate-ir.net/External.File?item=UGFyZW50SUQ9MjM0OTh8Q2hpbGRJRD0tMXxUeXBlPTM=&t=1).

[98] In 2008 and 2009, Intesa Sanpaolo issued €2.5 billion preference and innovative equity instruments, which contribute to Tier 1 capital (Intesa Sanpaolo Group Annual Reports 2009).

[99] Intesa Sanpaolo, "Intesa Sanpaolo signs agreement for sale of securities services business to State Street Corporation", press release, 22 December 2009 (http://www.group.intesasanpaolo.com/scriptIsir0/si09/contentData/view/content-ref?id=CNT-04-000000003F91A).

capital injection of up to €4 billion from the Italian Government, but decided in September not to opt for the plan due to its costs.[100] Under pressure from the regulator and supervisor, Intesa Sanpaolo announced in April 2011 that it would strengthen its capital by issuing €5 billion of new shares at the end of the year.[101]

Bank: UniCredit Group	Country: Italy

Activities. The listed financial group UniCredit Group is primarily engaged in retail and corporate banking in Italy, Germany, Austria and Central and Eastern Europe. In addition, the financial group also offers insurance products and has capital market activities, which mainly support the other activities. The group grew substantially in the second half of the 2000s due to its acquisitions, including HVB Group in Germany (2006), Bank Austria Creditanstalt in Austria (2006) and Capitalia Group in Italy (2007).

Crisis. UniCredit reported lower profits during the financial turmoil due to higher risk costs, lower trading income and write downs on investments.[102] UniCredit did not receive any state aid during the crisis, but had to raise capital by issuing share and hybrid instruments as well as retaining earnings.[103] In 2009, the bank announced that it was considering applying for government support, which would be costly for shareholders,[104] but finally (in January 2010) issued approximately €4 billion of new ordinary shares[105] to increase its capital level.

Capital requirements. Unlike other Italian commercial banks, UniCredit was granted extra time to raise its capital ratios to the capital requirements levels of Basel III. The deadline for the bank was postponed to end-2011 in April 2011, mainly because of its

---

[100] Intesa Sanpaolo, "Intesa has second thoughts over €4bn aid", Patrick Jenkins and Vincent Boland, Financial Times, 3 September 2009 (http://www.ft.com/cms/s/0/761c0790-98ad-11de-aa1b-00144feabdc0.html#axzz1LIiN5zY0).

[101] Intesa Sanpaolo, "Intesa Sanpaolo: Capital Increase", press release, 6 April 2011 (http://www.group.intesasanpaolo.com/scriptIsir0/si09/contentData/view/content-ref?id=CNT-04-00000000464EA).

[102] UniCredit purchased in 2007 Kazakh ATF bank for about €1.7 billion and had to write down in 2008 and 2010 about €0.8 billion on goodwill. In addition, the bank has stated impairments of €0.3 billion in 2008 on the acquisition of USB in Ukraine for about €1.6 billion a year earlier. (Sources: UniCredit Group (2007), "UniCredit: Bank Austria signs agreement to acquire majority shareholding in AFT Bank in the Republic of Kazakhstan", press release, 21 June; UniCredit Group (2007), "UniCredit: Bank Austria signs agreement to acquire majority shareholding in Ukrsotsbank in Ukraine", press release, 5 July; and UniCredit Annual Reports 2008 & 2010.)

[103] At the end of 2009, the Tier 1 capital of €39 billion included €5 billion of (non)-innovative capital instruments; €3 billion of this hybrid capital was raised in 2008 and 2009.

[104] Bloomberg, "UniCredit Plans EU4 Billion-Euro Stock Sale, Rejects State Aid", Sonia Sirletti, Bloomberg, 29 September 2009 (http://www.bloomberg.com/apps/news?pid=newsarchive&sid=a6uTR1DMel70).

[105] UniCredit Group, "The Board of Directors determines the conditions of the capital increase, subject to obtaining the regulatory approvals required by applicable laws", press release, 7 January 2010 (http://www.unicreditgroup.eu/en/pressreleases/PressRelease1379.htm).

fragile shareholder base, i.e. three major shareholders lack funds to participate in a rights issue.[106]

Bank: ABN Amro Holding	Country: The Netherlands

Takeover. ABN Amro is currently a state-owned bank, following the merger between Fortis Bank Nederland and the Dutch and International Private Banking of the former ABN Amro. In October 2007, ABN Amro was acquired for €72 billion by a hostile takeover of a consortium consisting of RBS, Fortis and Santander.[107] These three financial groups divided up the bank's activities. RBS acquired the wholesale activities; Fortis obtained the asset management and Dutch activities; and Santander bought the Italian and Brazilian activities.[108] In the fall of 2008, Santander's parts were de-merged while the Dutch state acquired the Fortis bank's parts. The break-up of the activities of the group was completed in February 2010 when the former RBS and Fortis parts were split.[109] In July 2010, the former Fortis part in ABN Amro and the banking activities of Fortis in the Netherlands were merged to form the new ABN Amro bank.[110]

Activities. The new bank focuses mainly on providing basic banking services to retail customers and SMEs in the Netherlands as well as private banking services to its international clients. Between the years 2006 and 2009, the bank's categorisation changed several times according to the results of the cluster analysis. Formerly assigned to the retail bank category, ABN Amro was re-categorised as an investment bank in 2008, owing to the break-up of the retail activities from the main group. The clustering assignment changed once again in 2009, when the bank was categorised as a wholesale bank due to the de-merger of the activities and sale of some of the retail activities.

State aid. Owing partly to its failed merger in 2007-08, ABN Amro has received substantial support from the Dutch government to increase capital and eliminate liquidity shortages. After the rescue and the subsequent break-up of Fortis by the governments of Belgium, Luxembourg and the Netherlands, the Dutch government bought the parts sold to Fortis (for €12.8 billion) and Fortis's Dutch insurance activities (€4 billion). In addition, the Dutch authorities provided liquidity facilities of €34 billion to

---

[106] Financial Times, "UniCredit given extra time on capital ratios", Patrick Jenkins, Financial Times, 20 April 2011 (http://www.ft.com/cms/s/0/0d2c3334-6aa9-11e0-80a1-00144feab49a,s01=1.html#axzz1JxU9WLTW).

[107] Financial Times, "Spanish in position", Victor Mallet, Financial Times, 20 October 2009 (http://www.ft.com/cms/s/0/53bc70a6-bda9-11de-9f6a-00144feab49a.html#axzz1HKuk3rbB).

[108] In an earlier stage of the takeover battle in 2007, ABN Amro already sold its US subsidiary LaSalle for $21 billion (€16 billion) to Bank of America. For more, see Financial Times, "$21bn sale of ABN's US arm finalised", Sarah Laitner, 2 October 2007 (http://www.ft.com/cms/s/0/db658146-7080-11dc-a6d1-0000779fd2ac.html#axzz1HKuk3rbB).

[109] ABN Amro, "ABN AMRO completes legal demerger", press release, 8 February 2010 (http://www.abnamro.com/en/press-room/press-release-archive/2010/ABN-AMRO-completes-legal-demerger.html).

[110] ABN Amro, "Completion of ABN AMRO Bank and Fortis Bank Nederland legal merger", press release, 30 June 2010 (http://www.abnamro.com/en/press-room/press-release-archive/2010/Completion_of_legal_merger.html).

repay the short-term debts and €16 billion to repay the long-term debts of the new ABN Amro.[111] The funding obtained from the short-term debt facility was fully repaid in July 2009, following the issuance of €14.5 billion worth of government-backed bonds.[112] [113] Furthermore, in July 2009 and January 2010, the government supported two recapitalisation plans of €2.5 billion (€1.7 billion via a capital relief instrument) and €4.4 billion to enable the breakup of the bank and to compensate a shortfall in capital due to the forced sale of New HBU.[114]

Bank: ING Group	Country: The Netherlands

Activities. The financial group ING is among the largest insurers in the world and maintains a substantial retail banking network in the Netherlands, Belgium and other European countries.[115] ING's insurance activities are focused in the United States, but the company also has significant market presence in Europe and Asia. In addition, the bank is engaged in corporate banking, asset management and capital markets activities. However, the scale of these activities is relatively small when compared to other banks that are categorised as investment banks by the cluster analysis.

State aid. The ING Group was hit relatively hard by the financial turmoil, which resulted in losses on investments and higher impairments in 2008 and 2009. [116] In addition, the capital also decreased due to repurchasing of about €4.9 billion own shares between June 2007 and May 2008.[117] In November 2008, ING Group received aid from the Dutch

---

[111] State aid NN 42/2008 - Belgium, NN 46/2008 – Luxembourg, NN 53/A/2008 – Netherlands Restructuring aid to Fortis Bank and Fortis Bank Luxembourg, C(2008) 8085, 3 December 2008 (http://ec.europa.eu/competition/state_aid/cases/227768/227768_1027866_42_1.pdf).

[112] The €34 billion to repay short-term debt to Fortis was repaid to the Dutch State by July 2009. The long-term debt facility was reduced by €6.5 billion through the sale of Fortis's stake in ABN Amro to the Dutch State. For more, see Dutch Ministry of Finance, "Fortis Bank Netherlands redeems €34 billion to the Dutch State", press release, 2 July 2009 (http://english.minfin.nl/News/Newsreleases/2009/07/Fortis_Bank_Netherlands_redeems_%E2%82%AC_34_billion_to_the_Dutch_State).

[113] Dutch State Treasury, "Assigned Guarantees", overview, 1 December 2010 (http://www.dsta.nl/dsresource?objectid=5693&type=org).

[114] Extension of procedure in State aid case C11/2009 (Alleged aid to Fortis Bank Nederland and ABN Amro) to cover the additional recapitalisation measures in favour of Fortis Bank Nederland and ABN Amro and temporary approval until 31 July 2010 (NN 2/2010 (ex N 429/2009) and N 19/2010), the Netherlands, C(2010)726 final, 5 February 2010 (http://ec.europa.eu/competition/state_aid/cases/230806/230806_1084698_239_1.pdf).

[115] The bank also maintains internet and telephone-oriented direct retail banking activities in several countries around the world, including Germany and the United States.

[116] ING Bank lost in 2008 and 2009 in total about €3.5 billion on its Alt-A Residential Mortgage-Backed Securities portfolio (RMBS) in the US. An additional loss of €7.5 billion on the portfolio was classified in 2008 as negative revaluation reserve, i.e. considered as a temporal loss provision. Due to the acquisition of 80% of the Alt-A portfolio by the Dutch government in 2009, the temporal loss provision could be reclassified as equity.

[117] ING Group, "ING completes share buyback programme", press release, 23 May 2008 (http://www.ing.com/group/showdoc.jsp?docid=323163_EN).

government to halt the immediate capital shortage. Initially, the group received a capital injection of €10 billion in non-voting equity securities and the state guaranteed bonds of $9 billion (€6 to 7 billion) and €5 billion. Subsequently, in January 2009, the state acquired 80% on the Alt-A and Prime RMBS portfolio in the United States for 90% of the par value which increased ING's capital ratios.[118,119] In December 2009, the group started repaying the capital injection of the state. In first instance the ING repaid half of the capital injection by issuing €7.5 billion in new shares.[120] In May 2011, the group repaid an additional €2 billion of the capital injection. One month later, the group announced they would repay the remaining €3 billion before May 2012.[121]

Restructuring. The restructuring plan approved by the European Commission has the aim to decrease the complexity and costs of the organisation as well as the riskiness of ING's activities in the period till 2014. Since then the complexity of the group has mainly been reduced by separating the banking and insurance activities. A large part of the insurance activities must be divested and the banking activities will reduce their risk profile by focusing more on traditional retail banking and generating more own assets, instead of buying securities. The bank also had to carve out a new retail bank with a substantial presence on the Dutch market to increase competition in the concentrated domestic banking market. [122] Under the restructuring plan, ING Group announced in June 2011 it would sell its subsidiary ING Direct USA for $9 billion (€6.3 billion) to Capital One.[123]

Bank: Rabobank Group	**Country: The Netherlands**

Activities. Rabobank Group is a fully integrated cooperative banking group focused primarily on retail banking activities in the Netherlands. The group is also engaged in

---

[118] State Aid C 10/2009 (ex N 138/2009) - illiquid assets back-up facility for ING, The Netherlands, C(2009) 2585 final corr., 31 March 2009 (http://ec.europa.eu/competition/state_aid/cases/230724/230724_958423_46_1.pdf).

[119] The total par value of the Alt-A and Prime RMBS was €30 billion, much higher than the fair value of €18.4 billion (December 2008).

[120] The European Commission requested the Dutch state to increase the guarantee fee paid and the management fee received by ING. The fees were adjusted in October 2009, i.e. the guarantee fee paid by ING was increased from 55BP to 137 BP per annum and the management fee charged by ING was decreased from 25 to 10 BP per annum. In total the bank used €1.3 billion of the issuance to cover an increase of the guarantee premium on the RMBS portfolio sold to the state.

[121] ING Group, "Background to the sale of ING DIRECT USA", press release, 17 June 2011 (http://www.ing.com/Our-Company/Press-room/Press-release-archive/Background-to-the-sale-of-ING-DIRECT-USA.htm).

[122] State Aid C 10/2009 (ex N 138/2009)-implemented by the Netherlands for ING's Illiquid Assets Back-Up Facility and Restructuring Plan, C(2009) 2585 final corr., 31 March 2009 http://ec.europa.eu/competition/state_aid/cases/230724/230724_1071446_207_1.pdf.

[123] It is worth noting that almost one-third of the takeover bid ($2.8 billion or €1.7 billion) is paid in Capital One shares and the remaining RMBS portfolio is excluded from the deal.

wholesale, asset management (Robeco) and insurance activities, owning part of the Dutch insurer Eureko.[124] The group's less prominent international activities serve mainly the agricultural sector and retail customers in Australia, New Zealand, United States, Brazil and Poland.

Crisis. Rabobank had to increase its provisions for bad debt amidst the crisis due to its real estate exposures in the Netherlands and Ireland.[125] Nevertheless, the financial results remained sound for the most part. Between 2007 and 2009, the bank strengthened its capital by issuing about €3.5 billion equity securities to members and institutions.[126] The bank was one of the first European banks to experiment with alternative forms of capital, issuing in March 2010 €1.3 billion Senior Contingent Notes (CoCos).[127]

Expansion. In the past several years Rabobank engaged in several international acquisitions. First, the group increased its existing stakes in the Polish BGZ bank in 2008 and acquired part of the assets and liabilities of two local US banks from the Federal Deposit Insurance Corporation (FDIC) in 2010.[128]

Bank: Nordea Bank AB	Country: Sweden

Activities. The activities of the Swedish financial group Nordea is present in the entire Scandinavian region, comprising Denmark, Finland, Norway and Sweden. In addition to its primary focus on retail markets, the bank also engages in corporate and investment banking activities as well as life insurance and pension products as secondary activities. The bank is partly state-owned, although the government's ownership stake has been declining.[129]

---

[124] In the light of the new more stringent capital regulations the bank reduced its stake in insurance company Eureko from 39 to 29%. For more details on Rabobank's engagement in Eureko, see the press release (http://www.rabobank.com/content/news/news_archive/086-RabobankandEurekoAchmeafocusoncommercialalliance.jsp).

[125] Rabobank is one of the largest actors in the Dutch real estate financing market. The bank increased its market presence in 2006 with the acquisition of a large part of Bouwfonds, a large property developer, from ABN Amro. Irish ACCBank, acquired by Rabobank in 2002, was heavily hit by the crisis in the Irish real estate market. In response to these developments, the Irish bank shrunk its customer loans by almost one-third, triggering support from Rabobank.

[126] Net increase of member certificates, capital securities and trust preferred securities between 2007 and 2009.

[127] The contingent convertible bonds issued by Rabobank will pay out only 25%, instead of 100%, of their par value when Rabobank's equity level falls below 7%. For more, see Financial Times, "Rabobank tests investor appetite", Jennifer Hughes, 13 March 2010 (http://cachef.ft.com/cms/s/0/5af435f6-2e0c-11df-b85c-00144feabdc0.html#axzz1HS5YETt6).

[128] Rabobank Group, "Rabobank acquires deposits, certain assets and liabilities of Butte Community Bank and Pacific State Bank", press release, 20 August 2010 (http://www.rabobank.com/content/news/news_archive/013-Rabobankacquiresdeposits certainassetsandliabilitiesofButteCommunityBankandPacificStateBank.jsp).

[129] In February 2011, the Swedish government reduced its equity stake in Nordea from 19.8 to 13.5%. The government stake stems from the creation of Nordea during the Swedish financial crisis of the early 1990s. The Swedish government has announced to further reduce the share in

Crisis. The impact of the financial turmoil on Nordea's profits was limited. However, the group's Danish arm has been heavily hit, due to the local real estate crisis. The bank was able to attract additional capital without government support by issuing in February 2009 €2.5 billion of new shares.[130] Despite the crisis, Nordea bought the troubled Fiona bank for €121 million, which was part of the state aid agreement for the small Danish bank.[131]

Bank: Barclays PLC	Country: United Kingdom

Activities. The listed financial group Barclays has substantial retail, commercial and investment banking activities, mainly located in the United Kingdom, United States and South Africa.[132] Nevertheless, trading remains the bank's primary area of activity which is mainly in the capital markets and derivatives transactions.[133] Barclays's retail banking consists largely of credit card and consumer lending business; in 2009 this income was equal to the total retail income in the UK.

Crisis. Despite substantial write-downs in its credit portfolio, Barclays remained profitable during the financial crisis.[134,135] This is mainly due to one-off gains on sales of subsidiaries and gains on acquisitions, such as its £ 2.3 billion (€2.9 billion) before-tax earnings from the acquisition of Lehman Brothers' North American businesses in September 2008. In October 2008, in response to strengthened regulatory capital requirements, Barclays issued new shares and mandatory convertible bonds for a total amount of £ 7.3 billion (€9 billion). In 2009, the bank increased its capital position further by retaining gains from the sale of several subsidiaries, including a £ 1.5 billion (€1.7 billion) net gain from the sale of iShares to CVC and a £ 5.3 billion (€6 billion) from the

---

the upcoming years.

[130] Nordea Bank, "Nordea has a strong capital base and will not apply for hybrid loans from the Danish state", press release, 24 June 2009 (http://hugin.info/1151/R/1324633/311177.pdf).

[131] *State* Aid N 560/2009 – Denmark Aid for the liquidation of Fionia Bank, C(2010) 7427 final, 25 October 2010 (http://ec.europa.eu/eu_law/state_aids/comp-2009/n560-09.pdf).

[132] In 2010, Barclays settled a dispute with US authorities for $300 million (€225 million). The US authorities investigated the compliance of Barclays with US sanctions and payment practices, i.e. the bank processed between 2000 and 2007 payments of countries, persons and entities subject to economic sanctions.

[133] The bank was, for instance, the fifth largest global issuer of collateralised debt obligations (CDOs) at the time the US housing bubble burst. For more information, see Reuters, Global ABS CDO issuance 2006 and 2007, Reuters, 20 April 2010 (http://graphics.thomsonreuters.com/10/04/GLB_GCDOV0410.gif).

[134] In 2009 the bank even recorded a record net income of £10.3 billion, mainly due to capital gains on acquisitions.

[135] After Barclays lost the bidding war for ABN Amro of the Fortis, Santander and RBS consortium in 2007, the bank continued its £2.5 billion share buyback programme. This is to minimise the effect of the shares issued to China Development Bank and Singaporean Temasek Holdings used to improve its ABN Amro take-over bid (Barclays PLC, "Withdrawal of offer for ABN Amro and restart of buyback programme", press release, 5 October 2007.)

sale of Barclays Global Investors (BGI) to BlackRock. Meanwhile, the bank acquired smaller businesses, primarily credit card companies.[136]

Bank: HSBC Holdings plc	Country: United Kingdom

Activities. The listed banking group HSBC Holdings has substantial personal and corporate financing activities in Europe (United Kingdom), Asia (Hong Kong, China), and North America (United States). In recent years, HSBC broadened its global reach further by expanding in several Eastern Asian emerging markets. The bank's broad international retail network serves as its primary source of funding, representing nearly half of its balance sheet. In turn, trading and interbank activities are much less dominant, explaining the bank's assignment to the retail banking model in the cluster analysis.

Crisis. HSBC Holdings reported lower profits during the financial crisis, mainly due to write-downs on credit securities and the impairment of goodwill from the acquisition of Personal Financial Services North America, leading to a recognised loss of $10.6 billion (€7 billion) in 2008. In addition, the bank also lost about $1.1 billion (€0.8 billion) due to its trading losses in relation with the Madoff fraud case.[137] These losses were partially offset by one-off capital gains on the sale of subsidiaries, including part of the group's French network to Banque Populaire in 2008 ($2.4 billion, or €1.6 billion). To strengthen its capital base further, HSBC Holdings issued $17.8 billion (€13 billion) new shares in April 2009.

Bank: Lloyds Banking Group plc	Country: United Kingdom

Activities. Lloyds banking group was created in January 2009 after the acquisition of HBOS. The group's operations focus predominantly on the retail market in the UK. The listed group also has wholesale banking, insurance, and asset management activities. Non-UK activities include offshore activities in the Crown Dependencies and Switzerland, retail business in Ireland, corporate finance activities in Australia as well as smaller European retail arms.[138]

State aid. In 2009, the banking group received state aid to cover its heavy losses, mainly due to its acquisition of the troubled HBOS, which had been active in the structured finance market and which relied heavily on wholesale funding.[139] In January 2009, the

---

[136] These acquisitions include the Russian Expobank, Indonesian PT Bank Akita, Citi's Portugal credit card business, UK Standard Life Bank and eGG'S credit cards UK.

[137] HSBC also faces a $6.6 billion (€4.5 billion) lawsuit for its potential involvement in the Madoff case, initiated by the court-appointed trustee Irving Picard, who was charged with recovering money for the victims. For more information, see http://www.ft.com/cms/s/0/2428b572-016c-11e0-9b29-00144feab49a.html.

[138] State aid No. N 428/2009 – United Kingdom Restructuring of Lloyds Banking Group, C(2009)9087 final, 18 November 2009 (http://ec.europa.eu/eu_law/state_aids/comp-2009/n428-09.pdf).

[139] Due to the financial crisis the Lloyds Banking Group plc reported substantially lower profits in 2008 and 2010. In 2009 the bank reported higher profits, due to a net gain of £ 11.2 billion on the

Lloyds Banking Group received a capital injection of £ 17 billion (£ 13 billion ordinary shares and £ 4 billion preference shares). In return, the government received a stake of 43.5% in the group. In March 2009, the preference shares were redeemed by the issuance of ordinary shares by the group. The government bought 43.5% of these new shares. Lloyds strengthened its capital further in November 2009 by issuing £ 22.5 billion (€25 billion) of capital, which allowed it to opt out of the UK Assets Protection Scheme for its bad loan portfolio, worth £ 260 billion (€290 billion). Once again, the UK government bought 43.5% of the £ 13.5 billion (€15 billion) of issued ordinary shares. In addition to these capital injections in which the state took a predominant part, the group received liquidity support under the UK Credit Guarantee Scheme and the Special Liquidity Scheme of the Bank of England.[140]

Restructuring. The state aid was approved by the Commission under the condition that Lloyds would restructure its activities before 2014. The restructuring package contains measures to increase the viability of the bank's businesses by reducing its risk profile, diminishing its reliance on capital market funding, and increasing the operational efficiency of the integrated HBOS activities. To increase competition in the UK retail market, the bank has to carve out and sell a full operational bank with over 600 branches in the UK.[141]

Bank: The Royal Bank of Scotland Group plc (RBS)	**Country: United Kingdom**

Activities. The Royal Bank of Scotland Group plc (RBS) is active in the retail markets, corporate financing and capital markets. The retail banking activities are mainly located in the United Kingdom (Royal Bank of Scotland and NatWest), the United States (Citizens), and Ireland (Ulster Bank). The international investment banking activities grew fast in the years preceding the crisis due to numerous acquisitions, including a partnership with Bank of China (2005), acquisitions of Charter One in the US (2004) and ABN Amro (2007).[142] The group's acquisition of ABN Amro's wholesale and trading activities is the principal driver of the bank's transition from a retail bank in 2006 into an investment bank in 2008 and 2009, according to the categorisation from the cluster

---

acquisition of HBOS and capital gains of £1.5 billion. The income figures included from 2007 to 2010 substantially higher impairment charges. A larger part of these impairments originate from the loan portfolios in Ireland and Australia.

[140] Lloyds banking group received at the end of 2010 liquidity support from governments and central banks for a total amount of £96.6 billion (End 2009: £157.2 billion). The current issued Bank of England government liquidity facilities, UK Special Liquidity Scheme facility and UK Credit Guarantee Scheme, will be maturing in 2012. By March 2011 the bank did not receive liquidity support from ECB or FED.

[141] In March 2011, the bank announced to start an auction to sell the branches. For more, see Lloyds Banking Group, "Lloyds Banking Group appoints advisers for project Verde", press release, 28 March 2011 (http://www.lloydsbankinggroup.com/media/pdfs/lbg/2011/Verde_Release280311.pdf).

[142] State aid No N 422/2009 and N 621/2009 - United Kingdom Restructuring of Royal Bank of Scotland following its recapitalisation by the State and its participation in the Asset Protection Scheme, C(2009)10112 final, 14 December 2009 (http://ec.europa.eu/eu_law/state_aids/comp-2009/n422-09.pdf).

analysis.

State aid. During the financial crisis, the group received extensive liquidity and capital support from the UK government and the central bank. RBS needed the support mainly because of its high dependency on wholesale funding, higher credit risks, and losses on structured assets as well as those arising from the acquisition of ABN Amro.[143] In 2008, the group tried to restore its capital base without government help by issuing £12 billion (€15 billion) of ordinary shares. In addition, the bank sold Angel Trains Group (net gain £570 million, or €700 million) as well as its stakes in Tesco Personal Finance JV (net gain £500 million, or €600 million).[144] Despite these measures the state had to intervene in December 2008 by acquiring £15 billion (€19 billion) of new ordinary shares and £5 billion (€6 billion) of preference shares, which were converted into ordinary shares in 2009. In 2009, additional state aid measures were deployed, amounting to £25.5 billion (€29 billion) worth of non-voting shares and £ 8 billion (€9 billion) worth of contingent non-voting shares in 2009. In same year, the bank took part in the Asset Protection Scheme (APS) to offload £282 billion (€310 billion) of bad assets, with a haircut of £60 billion (€66 billion). As a result of these measures, the state owned a combined 70.3% of the voting rights and 84.4% of the economic interest by December 2010.[145]

Restructuring. In line with the provisions of the Commission's approval of state aid, RBS will have to concentrate more on its core banking activities in UK retail and corporate markets, reducing its reliance on wholesale funding as well as global banking activities[146] by 2013. The retail and corporate banking activities outside the UK, Ireland and US and part of the wholesale activities will be sold or ceased. In addition, the group agreed to sell part of its UK branch network to Banco Santander (net gain £ 350 million, or €400 million) to increase competition on the UK market.[147]

---

[143] Since the burst of the financial crisis in 2007, the Royal Bank of Scotland Group plc had three consecutive years of negative annual net incomes, mainly because of rising risk costs and high write downs on goodwill, e.g. in 2008 the group wrote down £7.7 billion on the goodwill created by the takeover of ABN Amro, £4.4 billion on Charter One and £2.7 billion on NatWest.

[144] Royal Bank of Scotland Group plc, "RBS to sell 50% shareholding in Tesco Personal Finance to Tesco", press release, 28 July 2008 (http://www.rbs.com/media/news/press-releases/2008-press-releases/2008-07-28rbs-to-sell-50-share.ashx).

[145] The RBS group also used liquidity facilities of the government and central banks, e.g. RBS issued bonds under the UK Credit Guarantee Scheme.

[146] The Global Banking division has to reduce its risk-weighted assets by about 45% to £150 billion.

[147] Royal Bank of Scotland Group plc, "RBS agrees to sell its RBS England and Wales and NatWest Scotland branch based business to Santander UK plc", press release, 4 Augustus 2010 (http://www.rbs.com/media/news/press-releases/2010-press-releases/2010-08-04-sale-of-branches.ashx).

APPENDIX IV. RETURN ON ASSETS (%)

Nr.	Name	Country	2006	2007	2008	2009
1	Dexia SA	BE	0.60	0.48	-0.60	0.24
2	KBC Group NV	BE	1.41	1.23	-0.85	-0.86
3	Bayerische Landesbank	DE	0.39	0.04	-1.16	-0.68
4	Commerzbank Group	DE	0.39	0.41	-0.07	-0.55
5	Deutsche Bank AG	DE	0.53	0.43	-0.38	0.24
6	DZ Bank AG	DE	0.49	0.25	-0.36	0.22
7	Hypo Real Estate Holding AG	DE	0.35	0.15	-0.53	-1.49
8	Landesbank Baden-Württemberg	DE	0.31	0.08	-0.59	-0.29
9	WestLB AG	DE	0.35	-0.52	0.01	-0.21
10	Dankse Bank Group	DK	0.68	0.58	0.06	0.15
11	Banco Bilbao Vizcaya Argentaria	ES	1.71	1.69	1.28	1.07
12	Banco Santander S.A.	ES	1.08	1.20	1.03	0.95
13	BNP Paribas	FR	0.73	0.65	0.19	0.44
14	BPCE Group	FR	..	..	..	-0.04
..	Banque Populaire Group	FR	1.44	0.42	-0.07	..
..	Groupe Caisse d'Epargne	FR	0.97	0.29	-0.43	..
15	Crédit Agricole S.A.	FR	0.54	0.34	0.07	0.10
16	Société Générale	FR	0.84	0.18	0.35	0.08
17	Intesa Sanpaolo Group	IT	..	1.55	0.33	0.58
..	Banca Intesa	IT	1.34	..	..	..
..	Sanpaolo IMI	IT	1.07	..	..	..
18	UniCredit Group	IT	1.00	0.90	0.48	0.31
19	ABN Amro Holding N.V.	NL	0.31	0.17	0.15	-1.03
20	ING Group N.V.	NL	0.81	0.84	-0.11	-0.13
21	Rabobank Group	NL	0.49	0.53	0.47	0.43
22	Nordea Bank AB	SE	1.10	1.00	0.72	0.61
23	Barclays PLC	UK	0.72	0.58	0.30	0.84
24	HSBC Holdings plc	UK	1.19	1.03	0.37	0.30
25	Lloyds Banking Group plc	UK	1.24	1.13	0.17	0.10
26	The Royal Bank of Scotland plc	UK	1.05	0.52	-1.53	-0.16
	Retail banks		*1.06*	*1.01*	*0.32*	*0.26*
	Investment banks		*0.66*	*0.22*	*-0.09*	*0.07*
	Wholesale banks		*0.61*	*0.30*	*-0.42*	*-0.37*
	TOTAL		*0.83*	*0.58*	*-0.06*	*-0.02*

APPENDIX V. RETURN ON EQUITY (%)

Nr.	Name	Country	2006	2007	2008	2009
1	Dexia SA	BE	18.5	17.6	-69.0	11.7
2	KBC Group NV	BE	24.9	23.7	-19.6	-16.2
3	Bayerische Landesbank	DE	10.7	1.3	-44.1	-16.3
4	Commerzbank Group	DE	15.6	15.5	-2.0	-17.5
5	Deutsche Bank AG	DE	25.4	23.6	-18.0	13.7
6	DZ Bank AG	DE	19.1	9.7	-18.4	8.2
7	Hypo Real Estate Holding AG	DE	16.6	9.7	147.3	-116.6
8	Landesbank Baden-Württemberg	DE	12.5	3.3	-43.5	-11.6
9	WestLB AG	DE	14.9	-33.9	0.7	-13.5
10	Dankse Bank Group	DK	19.4	18.5	2.3	4.7
11	Banco Bilbao Vizcaya Argentaria	ES	31.5	30.4	25.9	18.6
12	Banco Santander S.A.	ES	19.1	19.1	18.1	14.7
13	BNP Paribas	FR	19.3	18.6	6.7	11.2
14	BPCE Group	FR	..	..	..	-0.8
..	Banque Populaire Group	FR	22.4	7.1	-1.5	..
..	Groupe Caisse d'Epargne	FR	25.6	7.8	-15.2	..
15	Crédit Agricole S.A.	FR	17.5	10.4	2.5	2.9
16	Société Générale	FR	24.2	6.0	9.8	1.7
17	Intesa Sanpaolo Group	IT	..	17.2	4.1	6.7
..	Banca Intesa	IT	21.9	..	..	..
..	Sanpaolo IMI	IT	23.8	..	..	..
18	UniCredit Group	IT	20.4	15.0	8.6	4.6
19	ABN Amro Holding N.V.	NL	11.9	5.5	5.9	-25.5
20	ING Group N.V.	NL	24.1	27.9	-5.1	-3.8
21	Rabobank Group	NL	9.2	9.7	8.5	6.8
22	Nordea Bank AB	SE	24.9	22.6	19.1	13.7
23	Barclays PLC	UK	26.1	21.8	12.8	19.9
24	HSBC Holdings plc	UK	19.2	17.9	9.3	7.1
25	Lloyds Banking Group plc	UK	36.9	32.2	7.8	2.4
26	The Royal Bank of Scotland plc	UK	20.2	10.8	-45.6	-2.8
	Retail banks		22.4	20.2	6.5	4.4
	Investment banks		21.1	3.1	-1.6	-0.2
	Wholesale banks		17.6	9.3	-4.9	-18.5
	TOTAL		20.5	12.8	0.2	-5.2

APPENDIX VI. EQUITY RATIO (%)

Nr.	Name	Country	2006	2007	2008	2009
1	Dexia SA	BE	3.3	2.7	0.9	2.1
2	KBC Group NV	BE	5.7	5.2	4.3	5.3
3	Bayerische Landesbank	DE	3.6	3.1	2.6	4.2
4	Commerzbank Group	DE	2.5	2.6	3.2	3.1
5	Deutsche Bank AG	DE	2.1	1.8	2.1	1.7
6	DZ Bank AG	DE	2.6	2.6	2.0	2.6
7	Hypo Real Estate Holding AG	DE	2.1	1.5	-0.4	1.3
8	Landesbank Baden-Württemberg	DE	2.5	2.3	1.4	2.6
9	WestLB AG	DE	2.4	1.5	1.3	1.5
10	Dankse Bank Group	DK	3.5	3.1	2.8	3.2
11	Banco Bilbao Vizcaya Argentaria	ES	5.4	5.6	4.9	5.7
12	Banco Santander S.A.	ES	5.6	6.3	5.7	6.5
13	BNP Paribas	FR	3.8	3.5	2.8	3.9
14	BPCE Group	FR	..	..	..	4.6
..	Banque Populaire Group	FR	6.4	5.8	4.9	..
..	Groupe Caisse d'Epargne	FR	3.8	3.7	2.8	..
15	Crédit Agricole S.A.	FR	3.1	3.3	2.9	3.3
16	Société Générale	FR	3.5	2.9	3.6	4.6
17	Intesa Sanpaolo Group	IT	..	9.0	8.1	8.7
..	Banca Intesa	IT	6.1	..	..	..
..	Sanpaolo IMI	IT	4.5	..	..	..
18	UniCredit Group	IT	4.9	6.0	5.6	6.8
19	ABN Amro Holding N.V.	NL	2.6	3.1	2.6	4.0
20	ING Group N.V.	NL	3.4	3.0	2.2	3.4
21	Rabobank Group	NL	5.3	5.5	5.5	6.3
22	Nordea Bank AB	SE	4.4	4.4	3.8	4.4
23	Barclays PLC	UK	2.7	2.6	2.3	4.2
24	HSBC Holdings plc	UK	6.2	5.8	4.0	4.2
25	Lloyds Banking Group plc	UK	3.3	3.5	2.2	4.3
26	The Royal Bank of Scotland plc	UK	5.2	4.8	3.4	5.6
	Retail banks		4.8	5.1	4.5	5.3
	Investment banks		3.1	2.7	2.7	3.8
	Wholesale banks		3.3	3.3	2.2	3.1
	TOTAL		4.0	3.9	3.2	4.1

APPENDIX VII. TIER I RATIO (%)

Nr.	Name	Country	2006	2007	2008	2009
1	Dexia SA	BE	9.8	9.1	10.6	12.3
2	KBC Group NV	BE	8.7	8.5	9.8	12.0
3	Bayerische Landesbank	DE	..	..	..	..
4	Commerzbank Group	DE	6.8	7.0	10.8	8.2
5	Deutsche Bank AG	DE	8.9	8.6	10.1	12.6
6	DZ Bank AG	DE	..	..	..	..
7	Hypo Real Estate Holding AG	DE	7.0	7.0	3.4	7.8
8	Landesbank Baden-Württemberg	DE	7.4	8.3	6.9	9.8
9	WestLB AG	DE	7.6	5.3	6.4	8.2
10	Dankse Bank Group	DK	8.6	6.4	9.2	14.1
11	Banco Bilbao Vizcaya Argentaria	ES	7.8	6.8	7.9	9.4
12	Banco Santander S.A.	ES	7.4	7.7	..	..
13	BNP Paribas	FR	7.2	7.0	7.9	10.1
14	BPCE Group	FR	..	..	..	9.1
..	Banque Populaire Group	FR	..	9.1	7.7	..
..	Groupe Caisse d'Epargne	FR	..	..	..	..
15	Crédit Agricole S.A.	FR	4.6	5.4	7.2	7.2
16	Société Générale	FR	7.8	5.5	8.2	9.9
17	Intesa Sanpaolo Group	IT	..	6.1	6.6	7.8
..	Banca Intesa	IT	5.8	..	..	..
..	Sanpaolo IMI	IT	5.9	..	..	..
18	UniCredit Group	IT	6.6	6.4	6.8	8.6
19	ABN Amro Holding N.V.	NL	7.9	10.9	10.9	19.9
20	ING Group N.V.	NL	7.6	7.4	9.3	10.2
21	Rabobank Group	NL	10.7	10.7	12.8	13.8
22	Nordea Bank AB	SE	7.1	7.0	6.9	9.5
23	Barclays PLC	UK	6.8	7.4	8.5	12.8
24	HSBC Holdings plc	UK	8.7	8.7	8.3	10.8
25	Lloyds Banking Group plc	UK	6.5	6.4	6.4	8.1
26	The Royal Bank of Scotland plc	UK	5.2	6.4	9.6	13.4
	Retail banks		7.4	7.9	8.3	10.2
	Investment banks		7.3	6.3	8.6	10.5
	Wholesale banks		7.1	7.5	7.7	11.0
	TOTAL		7.3	7.4	8.2	10.5